KENTU

Off the Beate

KENTUCKY

Off the Beaten Path™

by

Zoé Strecker

A Voyager Book

Old Saybrook, Connecticut

The prices and rates listed in this guidebook were confirmed at press time. We recommend, however, that you call establishments before traveling to obtain current information.

Cover: Gladie Creek Historical Site, Daniel Boone National Forest, near Slade, Kentucky
Cover and text illustrations by Richard Gersony

Library of Congress Cataloging-in-Publication Data
Strecker, Zoé.
Kentucky: off the beaten path / by Zoé Strecker.—1st ed.
p. cm.
"A Voyager book."
Includes index.
ISBN 1-56440-021-2
1. Kentucky—Description and travel—1981- —Guide-books.
I. Title
F449.3.S76 1992
917.6904'43—dc20 91-41393
CIP

Manufactured in the United States of America
First Edition/Second Printing

To those Kentuckians who, with lots of love and humor, continue to guide me off the beaten path in all realms of life

Contents

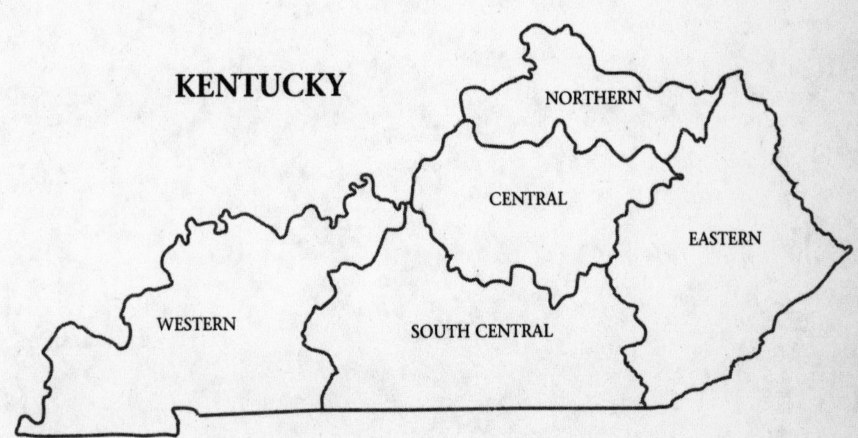

Introduction

In an age when "Vive la Difference!" is our cultural rallying cry, Kentucky should be a traveler's sheer delight. This forty-thousand-square-mile stretch of land is home to a greater variety of distinct cultures than any other rural state in the union. Our landscapes vary wildly, our accents fluctuate county to county, and we're downright contradictory, always have been. This contradictory nature is a quality that is both enjoyable and educational for locals as well as inquisitive outsiders. Despite being a longtime victim of simplified stereotypes, the Commonwealth of Kentucky doesn't include a single "typical Kentuckian." Where the edges of Kentucky's cultures overlap, delightful contrasts abound. Where else can you find hitching posts for horse and buggy rigs in a Druther's fast food parking lot? Where else do you hear English spoken with a heavy German lilt and a thick Southern twang? Or an Elizabethan dialect with a drawl?

Maybe the contradictions started with Daniel Boone (what didn't?), who was torn between settling the land he loved passionately and, not trusting his fellow pioneers, merging with the native people who loved and adopted him. Maybe Kentucky's contradictory nature proved itself in bearing both Civil War presidents into the world within a year and less than 100 miles apart. The same waters that produce the world's smoothest bourbon and worst bootleg also sustained the life of Carrie Nation and continue to fill the teetotalers' baptismal fonts. Stereotypes of illiteracy are at loggerheads with a remarkable history of erudition and fine literary accomplishments, and the lack of national recognition for Kentucky's contributions to the high arts is suspect upon examination of the state's almost unequalled tradition of music, dance, and fine craft.

Then there's our geography, as erratic as Colorado, yet older and more diverse in terms of flora and fauna. Vast, big-sky country dominates the western regions where acre after fertile acre fans out, making a flat, midwestern horizon, ending in swampland and rich arable bottomland by the banks of the great Mississippi and Ohio rivers. Central and Northern Kentucky ride on a high, fertile plateau where game has always grazed and where livestock continue to make the region wealthy and world famous for equine and bovine bloodlines. Eastern Kentucky's lush mountains are well rounded with age, well supplied with precious seams of coal and iron ore, and laced with clear, beautiful streams. The South Central region has a touch of it all, plus some of the world's most spectacular caverns.

In this book I'm just giving you leads to places that you may not have otherwise found. Your job is to immerse yourself and explore everything with fresh eyes and an open heart. The people here are so friendly, you'll get tired of smiling.

The pleasure of traveling in Kentucky begins with studying the map. Read the names of our towns and you'll begin to believe that this soil grows poets (and humorists) even better than tobacco: Bear Wallow, Horse Fly Holler, Cat Creek, Dog Town, Dogwalk, Dog Trot, Maddog, The Bark Yard, Monkey's Eyebrow, Possum Trot, Terrapin, Otterpond, Buzzard Roost, Pigeon Roost, Beaver Bottom, Beaver Lick, Rabbit Hash, Chicken Bristle, Chicken City, Ticktown, Scuffletown, Coiltown, Gold City, Future City, Sublimity City, Preacherville, Fearsville, Shuckville (population 7), Spottsville, Jugville, Blandsville, Pleasureville, Touristville, Wisdom, Beauty, Joy, Temperance, Poverty, Chance, Energy, Victory, Democrat, Republican, The Mouth, Mouth Card, Dimple, Nuckles, Shoulderblade, Big Bone, Back Bone, Wish Bone, Marrowbone, Cheap, Habit, Whynot, Pinchem Slyly, Mossy Bottom, Needmore, Sugartit, Hot Spot, Climax, Limp, Subtle, Geneva, Moscow, Bagdad, Warsaw, Paris, London, Athens, Versailles, Ninevah, Sinai, Buena Vista, Key West, Texas, Pittsburg, Omaha, Yosemite, Two Mile Town, Four Mile, Ten Mile, Halfway, Twenty-six, Seventy-six, Eighty Eight, Bachelor's Rest, Belcher, Brodhead, Oddville, Waddy, Wax, Dot, Empire, Embryo, Factory, Tidal Wave, Troublesome Creek, Vortex, Princess, Savage, Clutts, Decoy, Thousand Sticks, Gravel Switch, Quicksand, Halo, Moon, Static, Nonesuch, No Creek, Slickaway, Slap Out, Sideview, Nonchalanta, Fleming-Neon, Hi Hat, Go Forth, Alpha, Zula, Zoe, Zag, Zebulon, Zilpo, Yamacraw, Yeaddiss, Yerkes, Uz (YOOzee), Wooton, Tyewhoppety, Kinniconic, Willailla, Whoopflarea, Symsonia, Smilax, Escondida, Cutshin, Cubage, Dongola, Nada, Nada (NAdee), Nebo, Slemp, Se Ree, Gee, Gad, Glo, Guy, Ono, Uno, Ino, Elba, Ulva, Ula, Ep, Eden, Devil's Fork, Paradise, Hell'n Back, Kingdom Come, and Hell Fer Certain.

Off the Beaten Path in Central Kentucky

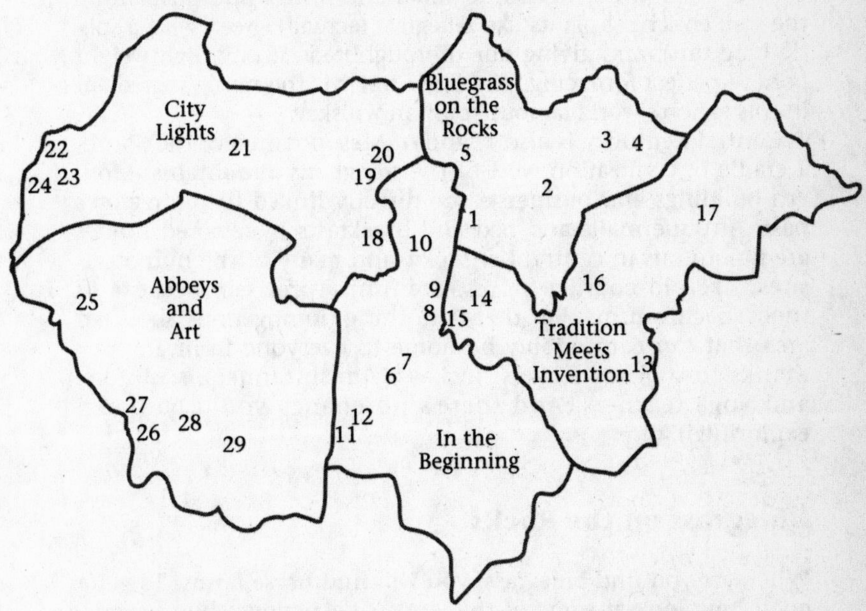

1. Headley-Whitney Museum
2. Kentucky Horse Center
3. Duncan Tavern
4. Cane Ridge Meeting House Shrine
5. Ward Hall
6. Old Fort Harrod State Park
7. The Beaumont Inn
8. Shaker Village of Pleasant Hill
9. Irish Acres Antiques
10. Nostalgia Station Toy Train Museum
11. Penn's Store
12. Perryville Battlefield State Historic Site
13. Bybee Pottery
14. Sargent & Greenleaf, Inc.
15. Highbridge Springwater
16. Hall's on the River
17. Ruth Hunt Candies
18. Wild Turkey Distilleries
19. Rick's City Café
20. Luscher's Farm Relics of Yesterday
21. Science Hill
22. J. B. Speed Art Museum
23. Kente International
24. Joe Ley Antiques, Inc.
25. Bernheim Forest
26. Abbey of Gethsemani
27. Kentucky Railway Museum
28. Rhodes Hall Art Gallery
29. David's Restaurant

Central Kentucky

Like nowhere else in the world, central Kentucky seems to have been created for horses. For this we can thank the rocks. Water percolates through the limestone strata and brings phosphates into the soil, enriching plants like bluegrass (actually green with a subtle blue tint), and giving our thoroughbreds strong, lightweight bones—perfect for racing. The same water is the magic ingredient in this region's world famous bourbon whiskey.

Central Kentucky is also a kind of Mesopotamia of the South, a cradle of civilization west of the Allegheny mountains. Modern buildings and businesses are directly linked to the region's past. Antique malls and bed and breakfasts in restored homes are ubiquitous in central Kentucky, and many of the humorous sites, like old country stores, are funny precisely because of their anachronisms. But there's nothing homogenous about an area that can comfortably be home to everyone from Trappist monks to soul food chefs, jockeys, Amish farmers, sculptors, and yoga teachers. And there's no chance you'll be bored exploring it all.

Bluegrass on the Rocks

Wherever you find bluegrass, you will find horse farms. To get a good long look at some of the world's best-known horse farms, take a drive on Harrodsburg Road, Old Frankfort Pike, Iron Works Pike, Paris Pike, Danville Road, or Versailles Road. Many of these and the smaller lanes that weave through them make wonderful bicycling routes. The miles of wooden plank fences are dizzying; these days most are sprayed with a black creosote-based paint instead of the traditional white. Dotting the countryside are ostentatious mansions and lavish horse barns where handmade wainscoating and brass chandeliers are not unheard of. Most of the farms are closed to the public, but there are a few exceptions. Three Chimneys Farm (606–873–7075) is open by appointment from 10:00 A.M. to 2:00 P.M. Take Old Frankfort Pike (Highway 1681) west into Woodford County and watch for the farm on the left after you cross Depot Road (Highway 1967). Spendthrift Farm at 884 Ironworks Pike is also open during the same hours (606–299–5271).

If you visit Spendthrift or The Kentucky Horse Park, stop by the Jot 'Em Down Store at the intersection of Iron Works Pike and Russell Cave Road. Once called Turrell's Grocery, this little store has been a favorite hangout for horse farm employees. Owner Robert Turrell remembers the late 1930s when his father and uncle listened for fifteen minutes every night to a radio show called "Lum and Abner," a comedic series about two store owners much like themselves. Lum was tall and savvy, while the Abner character was short, dim-witted, and funny. The fictional characters ran a grocery called the JOT 'EM DOWN STORE in Pine Ridge, Arkansas. The Turrells' customers got into the habit of calling them Lum and Abner and began adopting character names from the show, like Mousie and Grandpappy Spears. When the real Lum and Abner were in Lexington buying horses, they heard about the tradition at Turrell's Grocery, so they dropped in for a visit, bringing with them a sign that read JOT 'EM DOWN STORE. The rest is history. Come by for sandwiches and beers, and you may coax Robert Turrell into playing a recording of the old show—he knows every line by heart.

To see the most important aspects of the equine industry, go to the races and one of the big sales. Tattersalls Sales at the Red Mile is the number one standardbred sales company in the world. The sales occur throughout the year. Call for a sales or racing schedule (606–255–0752 or 800–354–9092). The Red Mile Harness Track has its racing seasons in the spring, late April through June, Wednesday through Saturday nights starting at 7:30 P.M., and in the fall for two weeks in mid-September and two weeks during the Grand Circuit season, which features afternoon races. Great trotters and pacers have been racing this track and provoking bets since 1875.

Across the street from Red Mile Road at 912 South Broadway (606–252–3481) is a small riding-apparel store called Le Cheval Ltd. Albert "Whitey" Kahn is considered one of the world's greatest tailors of custom-made riding apparel, with clients from coast to coast. The store is open weekdays during business hours. Even if you're not in the market for a fifteen-hundred-dollar riding suit, the fine designs are worth seeing.

Thoroughbreds alone brought over $300 million in Lexington sales in 1990. Fasig-Tipton at 2400 Newtown Pike is an enormous internationally known sales pavilion that is open to the public during auctions (606–255–1555). The Keenland Sales (606–254–3412) are similar, except that they're held at the Keenland Race Course at 4201 Versailles Road, near the airport. The Keenland Racing season includes two sixteen-day meets a year in April and October, the Blue Grass Stakes in the spring, and the final prep race for the Kentucky Derby. The races are big events carried out in deliberate, leisurely Southern style. Read the forms and watch your wallet.

As for tours, the track and some barns are open to the public year-round except in February. Go between 6:00 and 9:30 A.M. to watch workouts and then head into the track kitchen for a buffet breakfast (606–252–0406).

Just west of Keenland on Versailles Road is a castle surrounded by stone walls and mysterious rumors. According to the rumors a slew of celebrities have owned it, including Lee Majors. The truth is that the original owner and builder, Rex Martin, still owns the property but is looking to sell it. He and his ex-wife had the castle built to be a residence in 1969. Inside the turreted wall is a 10,400-square-foot, six-bedroom house complete with a huge library and swimming pool. Add chickens, goats, and peasants and you'd have a medieval village fort.

The bed and breakfast industry is rapidly growing in Kentucky in both rural and urban areas. Because new B&Bs are cropping up fast as lightning, you may want to call Central Kentucky Bed and Breakfast for an updated listing (800–225–TRIP). Presently there are several lovely converted houses open for lodging in the area. Rokeby Hall B&B is in downtown Lexington at 318 South Mill Street (606–252–2368). In Versailles, a few miles from Keenland, is the unique Shepherd Place B&B, in a pre–Civil War home with a great porch at 31 Hermitage Road, off Highway 60 (606–873–7843). In addition to being able to custom order handmade sweaters, hats, and mittens, you can meet the sheep face-to-face. Also near Keenland, at 270 Montgomery Avenue in downtown Versailles, is the Sills Inn B&B, a place with a reputation for its gourmet breakfasts (606–873–4478 or 800–526–9801).

Consider a man who was a jewelry designer known to drape diamond necklaces around the stubby red neck of his dachshund, Ernie, and then send the dog out to model the jewels for potential clients who were sunbathing at the swimming pool of the Bel Air Hotel. Try to imagine what kind of museum this man would build. When you give up, take a drive west on the Old Frankfort Pike to the **Headley-Whitney Museum.** Originally the late George W. Headley III established the space at his home to privately display his jewel collection, but in 1968 he and his wife opened the place to the public. The most famous part of the museum is the jewel room, which is filled with a bizarre collection of jeweled boxes and bibelots, small decorative objects made from stone and precious and semi-precious metals, most designed by Headley himself. The Shell Grotto is another odd aspect of the museum; supposedly George Headley installed the hundreds of shells himself. The main gallery area has a frequently rotating exhibition of traveling shows, regional artists' works, and private collections. Hours are 10:00 A.M. to 5:00 P.M. on weekdays and noon to 5:00 P.M. on weekends, except Monday from April through October, and except Monday and Tuesday from November through March (606–255–6653). Hint: The gardens are elegant for picnicking.

For more art, the Lexington Art League has its headquarters and a small gallery in the Loudoun House, a strange castellated gothic villa in downtown Lexington. It's an interesting place to explore and get a taste of the work of one group of visual artists in the area. From downtown go north on North Broadway and turn right (east) on Loudoun Avenue, then bear left when you reach a **V** in the road. Turn right onto Castlewood Drive. Hours are noon to 4:00 P.M., Tuesday through Friday, and 1:00 to 4:00 P.M. on weekends (606–254–7024).

A lesser-known art establishment in town is ArtsPlace at 161 North Mill Street, where off-the-beaten-path performances and classes are the norm. In addition to maintaining a gallery with rotating exhibitions of regional artists, ArtsPlace is the host of big, rip-roaring country dancing events the first Saturday of every month, plus modern and traditional dance classes, pay-by-the-session yoga classes, regular poetry readings, theater in the round, and noon music performances every Tuesday. Call (606) 255–2951.

A town this size has all manner of eateries, but there are a few special places, either oddballs or old standbys that you may miss. Buffalo and Dad's, near the corner of North Broadway and Loudoun Avenue, qualifies for both reasons. It's a quirky little hangout famous for its steaks and hamburgers, with a hoppin' bar scene, a sports- and horse-oriented decor, and a faithful crowd. Frank Adams (Dad) opened the place in 1979 and runs it with his son Robert "Buff" Adams, a big, burly fellow with a beard who deserves his nickname. Hours are 8:00 A.M. to 11:00 P.M. on weekdays; on weekends food is served until midnight and the bar closes at 1:00 A.M. Call (606) 252–9325.

What Buffalo and Dad's is to beefeaters, Alfalfa's Restaurant is to vegetarians. Actually Alfalfa's is not purely vegetarian, but it does emphasize meatless health food and titillating desserts. Come hungry. Saturday nights include live music ranging from jazz flute to Irish guitar. Alfalfa's is across from the main gate of the University of Kentucky at 557 South Limestone Street. They're open daily for lunch and dinner (606–253–0014).

Squeeky's Restaurant and Lounge on Newtown Pike, north of Third Street is one of those places that won't attract drive-by customers, but it should. It's a small block building with a suave cartoon mouse painted on the wall. Dinner is fantastic and inexpensive—barbecued chicken and pork, fresh greens, sweet potatoes, burgers, tangy slaw, cornbread, and drinks of all kinds. The jazz is even hotter than the barbecue sauce. Starting at 7:00 P.M. on Sunday and Wednesday nights, the Slim Jackson Band steals everyone's soul. Slim is seventy-eight years old, tall, and so thin you wonder if he can stand up. Then he starts drumming! He used to play with Red Fox, Sammy Davis, Jr., and other big names. Now he has gathered several Lexington jazz greats around him—Mike Allen, Miles Osland, and Jim Rankin. Jazz buffs should not miss this place. Call (606) 253–1088.

In the Chevy Chase area, at the east ends of Euclid Avenue and East High Street, you can eat cheap, good Mexican food on the patio or inside at Casa Galvan (606–278–8977) or get fine French pastries, made by middle-eastern hands, at Le Matin Bakery, 889 East High Street (606–269–1511). Down the street at 505 East Euclid Avenue, RamLata and Dinesh Saxena at the Indian Emporium carry everything imaginable from India or Pakistan—food, spices, religious objects, jewelry, gorgeous tie-dyed fabrics, traditional clothing, and even videos. In an otherwise ethnically thin city, this little place is a gem (606–254–3998).

To get an unusually intimate look at the world of thoroughbred training, plan to tour the **Kentucky Horse Center** at 3380 Paris Pike. From downtown Lexington take North Broadway out of town, which becomes Paris Pike (or Highway 68 and 27). After a few miles look for the horse center on your right. Since 1969 when this business was started, it has been one of the most prestigious privately owned thoroughbred training centers in the world. Over 1,100 stalls are leased to individual horse owners who bring in their own trainers and riders.

The tour takes you through a barn, along the rail, where you can talk to a trainer, and into the sales pavilion, where you'll be amazed at the complexity of yet another aspect of the business—horse sales. Tours take 1½ hours and cost $10 for adults, $5 for children. Available Monday through Friday, April 1 through October 31, tour times are 9:00 and 10:30 A.M., April to July 4, with an additional tour at 1:00 P.M. beginning July 5. Tour space is limited, so call ahead (606–293–1853). "Tracks" restaurant is on site and serves the usual Kentucky fare. Either before or after the tour, stop by the extensive tack shop where you may luck into an opportunity to watch leatherworkers in action.

We all love to experience a time warp. Even if you're not into bowling, stop by the Bourbon Bowl, south of Paris on Highway 68. This place has not changed since it opened more than thirty years ago. Owner Sue White swears she will never install automatic scoring devices or radically alter the decor. This place is super clean, and people say the snack bar serves the best cheeseburgers in town. Open bowling begins at 4:00 P.M. Friday and Saturday nights, and Saturday is "red pin night"—if the red pin comes up in your lane as the head pin and you get a strike, you win a free game and the admiration of your fellow bowlers.

Van Hoose Steak and Tavern is not only the most popular site for nightlife in Paris, but it may also be the best-loved steak house in the region. Owners Jon Marsh and Rudy Brown maintain the original owner's, Mr. Van Hoose's, tradition of serving fresh steaks only. The meat, which is never frozen, is cut in the kitchen, so it's as tender as a steak can be. There isn't a steak knife in the house, and their guarantee is "If the steak's not tender enough to cut with a table knife, you get it free." Prices are fairly reasonable, and the variety is good. After 9:00 P.M. on Thursday through Saturday there is live music, and on Monday and Wednesday nights the dart boards are open to the public. Go to downtown Paris on Main Street and watch for it on the right. The bar is open from 3:00 P.M. to 1:00 A.M., and the dining room is open from 5:00 to 10:00 P.M. every day but Sunday (606–987–6180).

Van Hoose would have had a serious competitor in the late eighteenth century when the **Duncan Tavern** on High Street was in its heyday. Major Joseph Duncan built the huge inn with native limestone in 1788, four years before Kentucky was a state. Everything else in town was built with logs, so the Tavern was an eye-catcher as well as a social catchall. Originally there was a ballroom, a bar, a billiards room, and a number of dining rooms, kitchens, and bedrooms. Today the Duncan Tavern and Anne Duncan House is a historic site owned by the Kentucky Society of the Daughters of the American Revolution, which has acquired enough period furniture and significant artifacts to fill the huge building gracefully. They maintain its tradition as a tavern by keeping it active as a party place. Daily (often twice a day), people use the Tavern for parties and receptions at no cost beyond catering fees. The D.A.R. hosts small events in the original dining room and serves meals on a long cherry boarding house–style table valued at $30,000. The Tavern is open to visitors Tuesday through Saturday, 10:00 A.M. to noon and 1:00 to 4:00 P.M. Call (606) 987–1788.

Another historic building being kept alive by means of regular use is the L&N Depot, between 10th Street and Winchester Road. Built in the early 1800s, this station saw lots of Civil War action, and Theodore Roosevelt is said to have made a whistle-stop speech here. Today it houses the very popular Iron Rail Restaurant, the self-proclaimed "Home of Home Cooking." For less than $5 you can help yourself to a large lunch buffet literally loaded with home-style foods.

From the transformed depot, you can take an anachronistic train ride behind a steam engine. Kentucky Central Railway (606–293–0807) runs trips from Paris north to Maysville on the Ohio River and back. Call for a schedule.

Bourbon County has more than eighty-five horse farms, but very few allow visitors. One fine exception is Claiborne Farm, which generously welcomes visitors by appointment only from 9:00 A.M. until 2:00 P.M. Call (606) 233–4252 or 987–2330. From downtown Paris, go south on Highway 627 (also called Winchester Road) beyond the edge of town. Watch for the farm entrance on your left.

The **Cane Ridge Meeting House Shrine** is the site of some powerful events and the source of some wild stories. Follow Main Street (Highway 68) north from downtown Paris and go east on Highway 460 to Highway 537 North. Take the latter for 5⁶⁄₁₀ miles and look left (west) for the shrine. Said to be the largest one-room log structure in the state, the church is impressive.

Two events made this church significant. The first was the Cane Ridge Revival in August of 1801, one of the nation's largest revivals during a period of big ones. Preachers stood on stumps and haybales all over the yard, talking simultaneously to 30,000 people for seven days and six nights. Women's hair stood straight out and crackled like fire. People spoke in tongues, barked, shook, danced, and were moved every which way by the Holy Spirit. The excitement ended only when the food ran out. The second event occurred in 1804 when the new Cane Ridge preacher, Barton Warren Stone, led the people away from the Presbyterian Church and started a new, nondenominational movement which, after linking with the Campbell movement in Virginia, became the Christian Church, Disciples of Christ. Today the denomination, which numbers nearly two million, owns and manages the shrine. In 1957 they erected an enormous limestone superstructure to protect the log structure. Later, a museum was built nearby. From March through October the whole place is open daily from 9:00 A.M. to 5:30 P.M. Call (606) 987–5350.

Near Millersburg, the next town to the north on Highway 68, an old but functional covered bridge called Coleville Bridge crosses the Hinkston Creek. Before entering Millersburg from the south, take Highway 1893 to the west for 3⅒ miles where you'll find an unmarked road going north (natural gas pipes are on each side of the road next to stone walls). Turn right and drive 1 mile to the bridge. If you tromp down the creek banks far enough, you can take photographs in which the graffitti won't show.

In Millersburg you can eat breakfast at 5:00 A.M. at Bridget's Restaurant on Main Street. She is famous for her homemade biscuits and gravy. Can't get up that early? Don't fret—*if* any are left, you can order biscuits and most other standard delights of country cooking from 5:00 A.M. to 8:00 P.M. On Saturdays folks around here sleep in, and Bridget's opens at 6:00 A.M. Next door is Ziggey's Pool Hall where you can eat pizza and shoot eight-ball as long as you can hold a table. Pool could be viewed as Kentucky's replacement for old-time legal dueling. Eat good food at Bridget's and settle your disputes at Ziggey's.

You'd better sit down for this one: the father of bourbon whiskey was a Baptist preacher. Apparently the good Reverend Elijah Craig ran a distillery, a fulling mill, a hemp rope walk, and a paper mill (the first in the state). According to legend, a fire swept through a building where barrels were being stored. Being something of a tightwad, Reverend Craig decided to put new corn whiskey into the charred barrels despite the damage. The color of the whiskey changed, the flavor mellowed, and a tradition was born. Eventually this new sour mash was named bourbon because large quantities were made in nearby Bourbon County. Baptists, don't despair. In the late eighteenth century Baptists were not overly concerned with temperance. Drunkenness among preachers was prohibited, but drinking was not. In fact, clergymen were often paid in whiskey. Gambling, dancing, and going to barbecues, on the other hand, were considered serious crimes.

Elijah Craig's sundry enterprises were all built near the Royal Spring, a very large limestone spring discovered in 1774. Georgetown was built around the spring, and the city still gets its water from it. The Scott County Historic Society maintains a park at the spring on South Water Street in Georgetown, the first major town north of Lexington off Interstate 75 or Highway 25. The information center is housed in an 1874 log cabin built by a former slave, Milton Leach. Call (502) 863–2547.

Downtown Georgetown is chock-full of history and is a good place for a walk. Fava's Restaurant, established in 1910 on East Main Street, is the place to eat lunch or have three o'clock coffee and argue local issues with politicians and merchants.

If you're interested in antiques, look in any direction. Three antique malls comprise more than 25,000 square feet of browsing space. The Central Kentucky Antique Mall, Wyatt's Antique Center, and the Georgetown Antique Mall are all on Main Street. The latter mall has a second entrance at 119 South Broadway that leads to another aspect of the business. Liz Cox does picture framing and custom leaded and stained glass work and creates what she calls family heirloom bears. The bears are made from vintage clothing, fabric, or fur that the customer supplies. Say your great-grandmother wore a fur coat that's been partially destroyed. Take the scraps to Liz Cox, and she'll transform them into well-made Mama, Papa, or Baby bears. Call her at (502) 863–2538. All of the antique malls are open from 10:00 A.M. to 5:00 P.M., Monday through Saturday, and 1:00 to 5:00 P.M. on Sunday.

If you're staying overnight, you have two unusual choices. Annette and Felice Porter's place, The Breckinridge House Bed and Breakfast at 201 South Broadway is an 1820 Georgian home much in keeping with the look of the town. It was once home to John C. Breckinridge, who ran against Abraham Lincoln for president. After losing, he became a Confederate general, married a Georgetown girl, and moved to this house. Two suites big enough to live in are offered to guests and include private bedrooms, baths, sitting rooms, and kitchens. For $60 a night, you also get an enormous breakfast. For reservations, call (502) 863–3163.

The Log Cabin Bed and Breakfast at 350 North Broadway is a fully restored 1809 log cabin, rustic on the outside, modern within. The large fieldstone fireplace is always ready with firewood for winter guests, and the porch swing is an enticing summertime treat. The cabin is equipped with a small kitchen, so extended stays are possible. Call Clay and Janis McKnight for reservations at (502) 863–3514.

One expects a lot from a house that took eight years to build, and **Ward Hall** is no disappointment. Prepare to view the ultimate example of the Greek Revival style. Built in the mid-1850s as a summer home for Junius Ward, the mansion has twenty-three rooms, five floors, two roofs, eleven mantels in Italian marble, four huge stone columns, and Sheffield silver doorknobs and hinges. The original exterior roof was copper and contained a kind of housetop cistern that made Ward Hall one of the first homes in the region to have running water. The tour is fascinating. From town, go west on Highway 460 and watch for the sign on the left side. May through October, the museum is open from 9:30 A.M. to 5:00 P.M. Monday through Saturday; it opens at 1:00 P.M. on Sunday. Call (502) 863–1619 or, to see about possible off-season tours, call (606) 299–1318 from November to April.

One of the best-selling cars in America, the Camry, is made exclusively in Georgetown at the Toyota plant on Cherry Blossom Way (Exit 129 from Interstate 75). Hour-long guided tours of the plant are given several times a day on Tuesdays and Thursdays. Call (502) 868–3027 for reservations. From an electric tram car you can see the Camry made from beginning to end. The place is mind-boggling—more than 4.45 billion square feet under one roof (a figure soon to double), overhead conveyors in perpetual motion, and robots everywhere, most doing body welding. One hundred and eighty cars are manufactured every day. Like it or not, this is industry.

In the Beginning

In the beginning there was Harrodsburg. A friend of mine swears that it takes a Harrodsburg resident less than four minutes of any conversation to bring up the fact that the genesis of the American West is Harrodsburg, Kentucky. On June 16, 1774, James Harrod and his company took a great leap of faith and of foot when they chose to settle the fertile strip of land between the Kentucky and Salt Rivers, more than 250 miles of wilderness and mountains away from the nearest Anglo-Saxon settlement to the east. Today you can begin your exploration of this significant historic area at a full reproduction of the 1775 fort in the **Old Fort Harrod State Park,** at the intersection of Highways 68 and 127.

Inside the park's entrance is the Mansion Museum featuring Civil War artifacts and the Lincoln Marriage Shrine, a red brick building that houses the log chapel where Abraham Lincoln's parents "got hitched." Inside the fort's walls, docents in period costumes demonstrate pioneer crafts during the summer. The fort is open to the public year-round, and from March 16 to November 30 the museum is also open from 10:00 A.M. to 6:30 P.M., daily. Admission is charged. Call (606) 734–3314.

Behind the fort is the James Harrod Amphitheatre, where "The Legend of Daniel Boone," a high-adventure drama, is performed under the stars from mid-June to the first of September, Monday through Saturday beginning at 8:30 P.M. For travelers with children, rest assured that this colorful drama easily qualifies as family entertainment. Call (606) 734–3346 for further information.

Across the street from the fort is The Gathering Place and the Fort Harrod Motel, owned by Marti and Forrest Williamson. In the summer months Marti entertains in the old-fashioned cabin she built for her collection of antique clothing, instruments, dolls, and myriad other domestic items. She sings and plays the hammered dulcimer, mountain lap dulcimer, autoharp, guitar, dobro, and folk harps. You can hear her perform Tuesday through Saturday from mid-June through the end of August. Regular programs are at 4:00 P.M., but check the sign on the door for other performances. Admission is charged. Call (606) 734–4189.

Follow Chiles Street south, one block behind the Williamson's place, to Kentucky's first row house, circa 1800, known as Morgan Row after the builder Joseph Morgan. The street is named after Morgan's son-in-law, John Chiles, who ran a famous tavern on the site. In front of Morgan Row, Uncle Will of Wildwood, a prominent Mercer County farmer, is said to have been cited for speeding in his one-horse buggy. When Uncle Will went to pay his ticket, he paid double the amount, telling the clerk in a voice loud enough for the whole courthouse to hear, "I'm paying you double 'cause I plan to leave the way I came."

Today Morgan Row houses the Harrodsburg Historical Society Office and museum, the Chamber of Commerce, and the Tourist Commission, where you can find additional historical information. Down the street is the Old Mercer County Jail building, which has been converted into a bed and breakfast. If the idea of sleeping behind bars strikes you as unappealing, stop in and take a look at the cheerful quarters. Call owner Carole Nichols at (606) 734–7012.

When Raymond and Sharyn Sirkle moved into the big, beautiful 1850s house at 367 North Main Street, they discovered it was inevitably described as "Ms. Jesta Bell's place" by local folks. Later, when they decided to open four rooms as bed and breakfast facilities, the name seemed a given. A well-loved woman in the community, the late Jesta Bell Matherly was a painter and an art teacher at Asbury College. The Sirkles have a few of her watercolors hanging in the parlor. At Ms. Jesta Bell's Bed and Breakfast, rooms with breakfast are $65 per night. Call (606) 734–7834 for reservations.

Another of Harrodsburg's claims to fame is **The Beaumont Inn.** The graceful brick Greek Revival building, constructed in 1845, was once a finishing school called the Greenville Institute, then Daughter's College, and later Beaumont College. It was converted into an inn in 1919 by Annie Bell Goddard and her husband Glave. The inn has remained in the family and is now managed by Annie Bell's great-grandson Chuck Dedman. The dining room serves traditional Kentucky-style meals that include two-year-old country ham (smoked and cured by the proprietor himself), fried chicken, corn pudding, and Robert E. Lee Orange-Lemon Cake. Be ready for a feast! The antique-filled sleeping quarters embody the extravagant beauty of the Old South, with a few modern conveniences. Swimming pool, tennis courts, and a gift shop are also on the premises. Reservations are advisable for meals and lodging. Call (606) 734–3381.

If your appetite is lighter, you can find a tasty meal and hear the local talk downtown at the White Cottage Restaurant, locally known as Shorty's, in honor of the cook who makes Harrodsburg's finest country ham sandwiches. The Blue Ribbon Deli on Main Street is another hot spot for lunch. Sue Gilven's homemade pies alone are worth a trip to town.

One of the most unique historical buildings in Mercer County is the Old Mud Meeting House built in 1800 by members of the

Dutch Reformed Church. As early as 1781 a group of Dutch settlers immigrated here and formed a community in which they spoke Dutch and worshipped as they did in the Old World. The church they built became known as the Mud Meeting House because its massive timber walls are chinked with clay, straw, twigs, roots, and gravel. The handsome structure, constructed "for the sole Benefit & use of the said Reformed Church forever," has long outlasted its little congregation. The church was restored to its original form in 1971. To visit the site, drive south from town on Highway 127 to the junction of Highway 68 (Moreland Avenue) and turn right. Follow Highway 68 until you reach Dry Branch Pike; turn left and look for the historical marker. To see the interior, get a key from the Historical Society office on Chiles Street.

If you leave town going northeast on Highway 68, toward Lexington, you will pass my alma mater, Harrodsburg High School, affectionately known as "Hog Town." This nickname harks back to the late 1820s, when hogs outnumbered county residents two to one, there were huge hog corrals, sales rings, and auction blocks on those same grounds. Our official high school sports mascot was a pioneer with a coonskin cap, but our proud rallying cry was "SOOOOOOEYYY!!!"

Exactly 1 mile outside the city limits, look on the right for Harrodsburg Pottery and Crafts, a picturesque 1866 Victorian-style farmhouse surrounded by colorful flower and herb gardens. The shop features a wide variety of works by regional craftspeople, hand-dipped candles made right in the shop, and herbal and floral wreaths made by the owner, Nancy Washington. With its scented candles and herbs, the showroom is always permeated by a wonderful aroma. This place is best known for hand-thrown, functional pottery made by Chris Strecker (my mother) and other regional potters. Whether you need dinnerware, wedding gifts, or just an opportunity to handle fine workmanship, this shop is a delight and a real find. Open daily. In January, hours are by chance. Call (606) 734–9991.

Continuing east on Highway 68, you pass the world's most beautiful house of mechanic work, The Stringtown Garage. Father and son, Big Jack and Lil' Jack Pearson, have transformed a cement block eyesore into a little paradise. If you like their vibrant flowers, just honk and wave, or stop if your car needs some attention. As you drive on, this part of Highway 68 brings you into real saddlebred horse country. The first large horse farm on the right, with black fences and yearlings in the front field, is Oak Hill Farm, which continues its tradition of breeding world-champion saddlebreds. If you haven't already been charmed by Kentucky's mortarless fieldstone fences, driving Highway 68 will give you the opportunity to fall in love with the miles of hundred-year-old fieldstone walls visible on both sides of the road.

Continue east on Highway 68 for 8 miles out of Harrodsburg and watch for the entrance of **Shaker Village of Pleasant Hill,** one of Kentucky's most significant historic sites, on the left. The restored village is a museum featuring thirty original Shaker buildings and more than 2,700 acres of manicured farmland (about half of what the original Shaker community farmed at its prime). "The United Society of Believers in Christ's Second Appearance" was originally founded by an English Quaker woman, Mother Ann Lee, who came to America in 1774 and claimed to be Christ incarnate (this time as a woman) to herald the prophesied millenium preceding the total destruction of the earth. The most publicized doctrine of the sect was the belief that members should remain pure by avoiding the World (non-Shakers) and all its ways, including the "disorderly" state of matrimony. Instead of procreating, the Shakers adopted orphans and accepted converts, which were plentiful during America's "Great Revival" period of Protestant faiths in the early nineteenth century. Shakers also avoided the World by remaining economically self-sufficient. From seeds to silk, their products were always of the highest quality and continue to influence modern design. The Shakers' utopia lasted more than one hundred years until the death of its last Believer in 1923.

The village admission fee enables you to take a self-guided tour through the buildings, which, like Shaker furniture, are renowned for their graceful, functional simplicity. The village offers fine southern dining and overnight accommodations in original buildings. Call (606) 734–5411 for more information, special programs, and reservations.

The Shakers traded goods with "the World" in large part by river. From the museum entrance, go east on Highway 68 about ⅛ mile and turn right onto a road where a sign indicates RIVER EXCURSIONS. This road, built by the Shakers in 1861, still accesses one of the most spectacular stretches of the Kentucky River. Known as the Palisades, the high Ordivician limestone bluffs change color with the time of day. The river excursions are 1-hour trips on a paddlewheel boat called *The Dixie Belle,* from which you have a perfect view of High Bridge, the first cantilever bridge in America, a miracle of engineering at the time of its completion in 1877. High Bridge stretches 1,125 feet and stands 280 feet high; it is still the highest two-track railroad pass in North America.

Heading east on Highway 68, look for a sign on the left for Canaan Land Farm Bed and Breakfast. Be kind to your shock absorbers and drive the gravel road slowly to the 1795 Benjamin Daniel House. The farmers and hosts are Fred and Theo Bee, any number of their five children who may stop in, cats, sheepdogs, goats, and a large herd of sheep. If you're willing to help, you can try milking the goats or pulling a few weeds in the garden. Work and antiquities aside, you need to know that this place has a swimming pool! Call (606) 734–3984 for reservations.

If you're traveling toward Lexington or the Versailles area, continue east on Highway 68. The road begins to wind dramatically as it descends into the river gorge, crosses the Kentucky River on Brooklyn Bridge, and begins another curvy climb. About a mile up you'll come to a narrow "holler" that contains the Shanty Hill Market—you won't miss it and you shouldn't. Years ago I stopped to buy a watermelon. The old proprietor proceeded to tell me "how God intended watermelons to be et. You cut yursilf a tiny little plug, fill 'er up with a pint of Evercleer (tasteless, 200 proof, grain alcohol), wait an hour, and slice 'er up. Lordamercy!" Don't worry, today you will find a mother and son team who sell seasonal fruits, antique junk, grapevine for wreaths, bunches of deep orange bittersweet, and scrumptious homemade sorghum.

Traveling north on Highway 68, turn west or left onto Highway 33 and follow the signs that lead to **Irish Acres Antiques,** in Nonesuch (population 343), a "downtown" comprised of the smallest freestanding voting building you'll ever see and a cluster of houses, one of which has the greatest number and variety of purple martin houses known to humanity (the resident must be a frustrated urban housing planner). Irish Acres Antiques is a not-to-be-missed 32,000-square-foot antique gallery and tearoom founded by Bonnie and Arch Hannigan and now run by their daughters Emilie Hannigan and Jane DeLauter. Two floors of what was once the Nonesuch School are gracefully crammed with antiques that range from affordable early American primitives to pricey Asian art, fifteenth-century Chinese laquered boxes, and nineteenth-century French country furniture. An ornate $37,000 French palace bed is among the treasures.

The school's old cafeteria has been converted into an elegantly whimsical tearoom called "The Glitz." Amid a fantasia of lights, grapevines, iridescent paper, and silver cherubim, you can enjoy a lavish four-course meal for $10.95. It's a good place to take your time, and not the best place for kids. Reservations are required. Lunch is served from 11:00 A.M. to 2:00 P.M. when the gallery is open. Gallery hours are from 10:00 A.M. to 5:00 P.M., Tuesday through Saturday. Call (606) 873–7235.

Get back onto Highway 33, which winds through lush horse farm country to Versailles (pronounced Ver-SALES). You can also get to Versailles by way of Highway 60 or Highway 62 (once one of the largest buffalo trails in the United States). From the landscaping and architecture in town, one senses an aura of the wealth and deliberate pace of the Old South. Downtown Versailles is full of well-preserved Federal and Beaux Arts homes, beautiful churches, and antique stores, one of which is Hillside Antiques and Gifts (606–873–7483) at 197 South Main Street; a lunch place, Café on Main, is upstairs. Quilts and Silks, at 135 Morgan Street, is a real treat for fabric lovers. This place boasts all kinds of quilts and weavings, but they specialize in Amish and Mennonite work and do custom orders. Hours are noon to 5:00 P.M., Monday through Saturday. Call (606) 873–0255.

For the toy train enthusiast, Versailles offers a once-in-a-lifetime opportunity to pore over the collection of Wanda and Winfrey Adkins, who have converted an old (1911 to 1932) L & N station into the **Nostalgia Station Toy Train Museum,** located at 279 Depot Street, a one-way street on the east side of Main. The Adkinses, who do repairs and will find rare parts, can tell you just about anything there is to know about model trains and antique cast-iron and mechanized toys. I didn't realize there are modern versions of the 1950s locomotives, boxcars, switches, coal cars, and crossing lights we played with every Christmas. Wanda likes to point out a wind-up Mickey and Minnie Mouse hand pump car, one of L & N's forgotten "cheap" toys from the 1930s when the company was struggling and a regular engine and coal car cost at least $32. Hours are Wednesday through Saturday from 10:00 A.M. to 5:00 P.M., and Sunday from 1:00 to 5:00 P.M. Admission is $3. Call (606) 873–2497 for more information.

For enthusiasts of full-size railroad artifacts, follow Highway 62 west to the Bluegrass Railroad Museum, Inc. in the Woodford County Park. On weekends from mid-May to early November, you can take an 11-mile train ride on the Old Louisville Southern Mainland through quintessential Bluegrass country, including a hawk's view of the Kentucky River palisades. Call (606) 873–2476 for times, rates, and special events.

On weekends when you want a worthwhile excuse for a real country drive, visit the restored Jack Jouett House, circa 1797. This beautiful home was built by folks who believe, like Mies Van Der Rohe, that "God hides in details." Take Highway 1964 south and turn on Craig Creek Road. It is open on Saturday from 10:00 A.M. to 4:00 P.M., on Sunday from 2:00 to 4:00 P.M., or by appointment. Call (606) 873–7902 for more information.

From Versailles, take Highway 62 north to Midway, a town midway between Frankfort and Lexington. The first town in Kentucky built by a railroad company, these days it is a quaint college town full of antique shops, beautiful historic homes, and a few surprises. Don't miss the small jewelry shop called Lee Design at the east end of Main Street. The humble storefront belies the quality of the craftsmanship of the owners, art jewelers, Robert E. and Susan Lee. Ask to see the pin in rose sapphire, ebony, and gold that won an international award. Known for doing fine custom work, the Lees can be reached at (606) 846–4553.

You can choose from several eateries around Midway. For an inexpensive home-style lunch, try the Market Café on Main Street. The place is known for fresh chicken salad, a recipe that begins with boiling and plucking the chicken! The nature of "home-style cooking" depends upon what kind of place you call home. For those with a grander upbringing, lunch at the Holly Hill Inn may be "just like Mom used to make it." From Main Street, turn east on Highway 62, also called Winter Street, veer to the right at the Corner Grocery, and go about ¼ mile. The Holly Hill Inn, a Greek Revival home, circa 1830, was restored earlier this century in Victorian style and recently restored again and decorated in the original Greek Revival colors and styles. Two double rooms are available for $50 per night, breakfast included. The hosts and cooks are Rose and Rex Lyons. Open all year, Tuesday-Saturday, with lunch from 11:30 A.M. to 2:00 P.M. and dinner from 5:30 P.M. to 9:00 P.M. Call (606) 846–4732 for reservations.

Another gem near Midway is a century-old hydropower grain mill on the South Elkhorn Creek. The Weisenberger Mill is the oldest continuously operating mill in Kentucky and one of the few in the nation that has remained in the same family. In 1866 a German steamboat and mill specialist named August Weisenberger bought the mill that had been built on the site in 1818. He revamped the entire system and began grinding all manner of grain at the rate of one hundred barrels a day. His great-grandson Philip J. Weisenberger and Philip's son, Mac, have modernized some of the methods and now grind about 3,000 tons of grain a year. Although visitors are not allowed inside the work area, you can walk around the property. Everything Weisenberger mills is sold by the package in the front office (the fifty-pound bags are a very good buy). As an addicted bread-maker, I can attest to the excellent quality of their products.

Danville is a handsome little college town south of Harrodsburg. From Harrodsburg, take Highway 127; from Shakertown, take Highway 33 through Burgin. Drive or walk around Danville and the Centre College campus to admire the architecture. For arts and cultural events, check the gallery and schedule of performances at the Frank Lloyd Wright-style Regional Arts Center on campus.

You know an Italian place is good when there's always a customer at the counter reading an Italian newspaper. Freddie's Restaurant (606–236–9884) at 126 South Fourth Street serves quick, delicious, authentic Italian cuisine—primo for lunch and dinner on weekdays. If you're bicycling, this is a fantastic place to stock up on your "carbs." Stop by Dave's Bike Shop (606–236–9573) near Freddie's at 130 South Fourth Street for parts, water bottles, and directions to the lovely bike routes in this area.

The hospital in Danville was named for local medical hero Ephraim McDowell, who performed the first successful removal of an ovarian tumor in 1809. Something should be named for his patient, Jane Todd Crawford, who survived the surgery without the aid of antisepsis or the comfort of an anesthetic. The site of the operation, The Ephraim McDowell House and Apothecary at 125 South Second Street, has been accurately restored and is open daily from 10:00 A.M. to noon and 1:00 to 4:00 P.M.; Sundays from 2:00 to 4:00 P.M. Call (606) 236–2804.

Across the street is Constitution Square State Park, a reproduction of the state's first courthouse square and the site of the first post office in the West, established about 1792. All the buildings are log replicas and most are rigged with push-button recordings that allow you to enjoy a self-guided tour. The lawn is a good place for a downtown picnic, and dessert is right across the street at Burke's Bakery at 116 West Main (606–236–5661). Burke's is in its fourth generation of owners and customers. They make good old sweet pastries for those times when you just don't want whole grains and carob powder.

The Tea Leaf at 230 West Broadway is strictly for lunch, tea, and gift-buying. Rosemary Hamblin and Jane Stevens have specialized in children's books and adult aromas—it's easy to get carried away sniffing teas. Call them at (606) 236–7456. The Historic Danville Antique Mall, 158 North Third Street is housed in a large brick Presbyterian Church, circa 1867, across the street from the public library. The booths are full of old goodies, and hours are Tuesday through Saturday from 10:00 A.M. to 5:00 P.M. and Sunday from 1:00 to 5:00 P.M.

Danville has two bed and breakfast facilities. The Empty Nest (606–236–3339) wins the prize for the most honest name of the century. The house, located at 111 East Lexington Avenue, is in a perfect place for becoming overwhelmed with dogwoods, redbuds, and spring beauties in April. The Cottage at 2826 Lexington Road is a cozy farmhouse in rural Boyle County. Make reservations with Chris or Rube Kubale at (606) 236–9642. Also, the Bed and Breakfast Alliance of Kentucky has its office in Danville at 204 West Main Street. You can get listings and make reservations for B&Bs all over the state. Call (606) 236–1430 for current information.

If you're like me, your favorite nights during childhood were spent in a great-aunt's squeaky old cherry bed with tall, curving posts topped with balls or acorns. Brenda Lovett Phillips's passion for traditional furniture goes beyond mere nostalgia; her Junction City store, Lovett's Cherry Shop, is chock-full of walnut and cherry reproductions. People come great distances to pick up furniture orders from Lovett's—you'll understand why if you run your fingers over the satiny finish of a cherry lingerie chest. Follow Highway 127 (Fourth Street) south to Junction City. A few hundred yards past the road to the airport, Lovett's is on the left. Hours are Monday through Saturday from 10:00 A.M. to 5:00 P.M. Call (606) 854–3857.

Get apples big as a giant's fist, 50-pound bags of sweet Vidalia onions 5 inches in diameter, or tender green beans ANY season of the year at Lear's Produce, south of Lovett's on Highway 127 at the junction with Highway 300. Look for the sign that says LEAR'S PRODUCE: MATERS, TATERS, NANNERS & SECH, APPLES, KUNTRY SARGUM, PURHONEE. This place is a joy to behold in a world where the produce managers in big-time grocery stores seem to have been taught that repetition is the spice of life. Open Monday through Saturday from 9:00 A.M. to 6:00 P.M.

Leave Junction City on Highway 37 south. You have suddenly entered "the knobs," a narrow belt of fairly isolated wooded hills that encircles the bluegrass region. (Rock lovers: The creeks here are loaded with geodes.) In the heart of this alluring terrain is a little town called Forkland where there's a good little country festival the second weekend of October at the Forkland Community Center. Notice the huge, round piece of sandstone in the yard. It measures 51 inches in diameter, is 18 inches thick, and probably weighs over a ton. What in tarnation is it? No one knows. Sandstone is never used for grinding grain, so it can't have been a millstone. Archaeologists say it's not prehistoric. The best guess is that it was a "hemp brake," a heavy rock rolled by hand or by oxen over hemp stalks to break the fibers apart for making rope.

Near Forkland, **Penn's Store** may be the oldest continuously operated one-family-owned store west of the Alleghenies—and it looks it. Everyone falls in love with the wise, tumbledown appearance of Haskell "Hack" Penn's general store. In the winter the little coal stove is blazing hot and at least three men are playing checkers on a barrel in the middle of the room at all times. (It takes two to play and one to shake his head and chew on his toothpick.) In the summer there's no better place in the world to have a Dr. Pepper than on Penn's front porch where you can hear the creek rumble by. Hack's granddaddy, Dick Penn, opened the store in 1852. The original building burned; this replacement is more than one hundred years old. From Forkland, continue on Highway 37 to Highway 243, then turn right and drive a short distance. At the next intersection, take Highway 1856 to the left (west) and you'll see the store by the creek.

Leaving Danville to the west, Main Street becomes Highway 150 and leads to the historic town of Perryville. Under the shade of massive maple and sweet gum trees on the banks of the Chaplain River is a quiet haven made ready for rest and high tea. The Elmwood Inn is a well preserved Greek Revival home that has been everything from a hospital (during the Battle of Perryville), a private school, a music academy, and a restaurant. (Stains on my prom dress remind me of my first meal in the building as a nervous adolescent eating fried chicken.) The inn is now a stately bed and breakfast and tea room. Hostess and cook Shelly Richardson fills the ever-changing menu with traditional English delicacies like scones, chocolate raspberry layer cakes, quiches, and tea, of course. Reservations are expected for lodging or for tea, which is served every day except Sunday and Wednesday from 2:00 to 4:00 P.M. Call (606) 332–2400 to put your name on the list.

Across the river from the inn, you can see the back of Merchant's Row, a small strip of renovated buildings that house antique and gift shops, a pizza place, a dry goods store, and an active saddlery. Moving away from creature comforts, proceed in an appropriate somber spirit to the **Perryville Battlefield State Historic Site.** Go north on Highway 1920 for 3 miles and follow the signs. Forty thousand men fought for one bloody day on this site on October 8, 1862, when Confederate soldiers in search of water accidentally encountered Union troops who were guarding nearby Doctor's Creek. More than 6,000 soldiers were killed, wounded, or missing by sunset. A small museum with artifacts and battle displays is on the grounds, which offer plenty of room for picnicking. The best time to visit is during the weekend closest to October 8, for a massive annual reenactment of the long, gory battle. Reenacters wear full period costume and use period weapons. The park is open from April through October, daily from 9:00 A.M. to 5:00 P.M., and by appointment from November through March. Call (606) 332–8631 for more information.

The William Whitley House State Historic Site is southeast of Stanford on Highway 150. Famous Indian Fighter (a dubious claim to fame) William Whitley built the elegant brick house in the mid-1780s. Probably the oldest brick building west of the Alleghenies, it was called "a guardian of the Wilderness Road" because it stood next to the important overland route and served as a place of refuge for white travelers. The high upper windows and barred lower windows, gun ports, and a hidden staircase were built as precautions against Indian attacks.

Whitley's contributions to Kentucky (and American) culture were building the first horse-racing track in the state and racing the horses counterclockwise, a practice he encouraged in order to defy the British custom of racing clockwise. Having served as a colonel in the Revolution, Whitley was passionately anti-British. I'm sure he hated crumpets and tea. Whitley died in the 1813 Battle of Thames after he supposedly killed the great chief Tecumseh. Tours of his home are given from June through August, daily from 9:00 A.M. to 5:00 P.M. From September to May the home is closed on Monday. Call (606) 355–2881 for further information.

North of Lincoln and east of Boyle counties is Garrard County, birthplace of a radical antiliquor activist oft neglected by history books. From Lancaster, take Highway 27 north to Highway 34; go east to its junction with Fisher Ford Road to find Carrie A. Nation's birthplace at "the jumping off place," as local folks call it. The house was built around 1840 and Carrie was born there in 1846. In 1900, after a short, disastrous, and life-changing marriage to a severe alcoholic, Carrie single-handedly wreaked havoc on the saloon at the Hotel Casey in Wichita, Kansas, and, consequently, spent seven days in jail, her first of over thirty jail sentences on similar charges. I've seen fearsome pictures of Ms. Nation in her prime, hatchet in one hand, Bible in the other, purse to the front (the way one wears a pouch-wallet in Manhattan today), and a glare that would make any bartender's blood run cold.

If you choose to go southeast toward Berea, take Highway 52 from Lancaster to Paint Lick on the Madison County border, a don't-blink-or-you'll-miss-it town with one good reason to stop—Wilson's Hill Farm Baskets. Hugh Wilson, farmer of hybrid tobacco seed, hand-selects trees from land in the area and splits the wood, primarily white ash, into ribbonlike strips that are woven by Elizabeth Wilson into a variety of baskets. "People walk in here and are surprised to see how young we are. They expect to find old ladies sitting on a porch," Elizabeth says, laughing. She specializes in Shaker reproductions, but she also takes custom orders. Hours are 9:00 A.M. to 4:00 P.M. on weekdays and on Saturdays by appointment. Call the Wilsons at (606) 925–2386.

Tradition Meets Invention

Berea is a nationally known folk arts and crafts center located in southern Madison County off Interstate 75 at Exit 76. Stop by the Tourist Commission at 201 North Broadway for brochures about all the craft businesses. You can also call (606) 986–2540. You'll find more than thirty craftspeople in Berea—chair makers, potters, leathersmiths, blacksmiths, stained glass folks, weavers, spoonmakers, basket weavers, quilters, and others—whose studios and salesrooms are open to the public. Ask about the big outdoor fairs at the Indian Fort Theatre sponsored by the Kentucky Guild of Artists and Craftsmen.

An elegant place for fine regional foods and downtown lodging is the Boone Tavern Hotel and Dining Room (606–986–9358), owned and run by Berea College. Open daily for all meals, the restaurant has a dress code for evening meals. Berea College is a highly acclaimed liberal arts college that primarily serves low-income students from southern Appalachia. Students pay no tuition, but work ten to fifteen hours a week at any of 138 college-owned businesses, which include the Boone Tavern and studios for pottery, weaving, woodworking, broom-making, etc. The student-made crafts are sold at the Log House Sales Room on Jackson Street. The college also runs the Appalachian Museum, near the Tavern; it features mountain life artifacts and craft demonstrations. Call (606) 986–9341, extension 6078 for hours and information.

North of Berea is Richmond, home of Eastern Kentucky University. Very much a university town, it is full of restaurants, bars, hotels, and shops. If you plan to be in the downtown area at night, check the Phone 3 Lounge on First Street for live music, including acoustic folk/rock. For the stargazer, the Hummel Space Theater on Kit Carson Drive (on campus) is totally cosmic. The tenth largest planetarium in the nation, it seems enormous as you crane your neck in the dark dome to catch a view of the galaxy 9.3 billion miles away from Earth. Shows are Wednesday through Saturday nights at 7:30 or Saturday and Sunday afternoons at 3:30. Call (606) 622–1547.

Five generations of Cornelisons have kept **Bybee Pottery** thriving since at least 1845, making it the oldest existing pottery west of the Alleghenies. If you're from this region, you've probably seen Bybee's pots in homes of all kinds. The wheel-thrown, slip-cast (molded), and jiggered stoneware pots are based on traditional designs. Glaze colors and application methods are as they always have been, and the tools for every stage of the process have been modernized to a very slight degree. The charming droop of the studio building itself reflects the age and traditional nature of the pottery. The clays used in all of Bybee's pieces (more than 125,000 annually) come from a small, remarkably pure clay mine less than 2 miles away. Visitors are welcome to mosey around the entire work area. Take Highway 52 east from Richmond for 9 miles. The Bybee salesroom and workshop are open on weekdays from 8:00 A.M. to noon and from 12:30 P.M. to 4:30 P.M. Call (606) 369–5350.

The White Hall State Historic Site is accessible from Interstate 75 (Exit 90) or directly from Richmond. Take Highway 421/25 and follow the signs to the restored home of one of Kentucky's best-loved big mouths and influential abolitionists, Cassius Marcellus Clay, the "Lion of Whitehall." White Hall is well fortified in part because Clay's ideological and political opponents were not beyond attempts at physically sabotaging the basement press on which he produced his radical paper, *The True American*. After the failure of his political career, Clay served under President Lincoln as minister to the court of Czar Alexander II at St. Petersburg, Russia. Later he retired and lived bankrupt at White Hall until his death in 1903. His home is open from April to Labor Day, daily, and from Labor Day to October on Wednesday through Sunday from 9:00 A.M. to 5:00 P.M. An outdoor drama called "The Lion of Whitehall" is presented on the grounds from the end of June through early August on Friday and Saturday at 8:00 P.M. Call (606) 623–0759 for further information.

Fort Boonesboro State Park is on the beaten path and self-explanatory. From Interstate 75, take Exit 95 onto Highway 627 and follow the signs. The reconstructed fort is at the site of Kentucky's second settlement. Interpreters at the park dress in period clothing and demonstrate pioneer crafts like lye soapmaking. Hours from April to Labor Day are 9:00 A.M. to 5:30 P.M., daily. During the rest of the year the park is only open Wednesday through Sunday. Call (606) 527–3131 for other information.

The Virginia Assembly granted The Valley View Ferry a "perpetual and irrevocable franchise" in 1785. Let me emphasize the word *perpetual*. More than 200 years later, the little boat is still carrying anyone and anything that needs to cross the Kentucky River on Highway 169 between Madison and Jessamine counties. The strangest passengers of late have been two wolves and a bear (nonunion movie stars). The governments of Jessamine, Madison, and Fayette counties recently decided to purchase and jointly operate this sole functioning ferry on the Kentucky River.

Locksmiths take note: The world's largest privately owned lock collection is housed in Nicholasville in the lobby of **Sargent & Greenleaf, Inc.** in the Jessamine Industrial Park south of town on Main Street (Highway 27). The collection belongs to Harry Miller, former president of the company, whose career, which began at the age of twelve as a locksmith's apprentice, eventually led to developing locks for highly classified U.S. government materials. While the State Department sent him all over the world beginning in 1940, he collected an amazing variety of locks in order to study their design.

The oldest lock in the lobby dates to 1303 and has Arabic writing carved into its decorative face. A lock taken from the White House's Oval Office during Lincoln's presidency and a key to the Capitol's sixteen-ton Columbus doors are in the collection, as are many of Miller's own invention; he holds fifty-four lock-related patents and hasn't stopped thinking about improvements. One of his outstanding inventions is the manipulation-proof combination lock. The collection is primarily admired by locksmiths on vacation and is frequently used by engineers and intelligence people for research in design. Because he sees the collection as "a history of man's ingenuity," he has given portions of it to the Smithsonian and has made the rest available to the public free of charge on weekdays from 8:00 A.M. to 5:00 P.M.

Kentucky ingenuity never ceases to amaze me. Upon leaving **Highbridge Springwater** and Kentucky Underground Storage, Inc., all I could think was, "That vault is as big as my farm!" Thirty-two acres of 30-foot-high limestone corridors 130 feet underground, high on the palisades of the Kentucky River, were originally created by the Kentucky Stone Company, which mined the area between 1900 and 1972. The Civil Defense Department had stored equipment and food in the cavern during the bomb-shelter era, mushrooms were grown here, and local hearsay is that the Free Masons conduct rites in the unused, unlighted recesses of the mine. In 1979 when Bill Griffin bought the property to use as an underground commodity storage area, engineers advised him to drain the water from an underground spring in order to control humidity. One day Mr. Griffin said to his daughters, "Well, why don't we just bottle the stuff?" Everyone laughed, but by 1990 the family-run business sold more than two million gallons of tasty, salt-free drinking water all over the state.

The water flows from what looks like a smallish spring 1,400 feet from the mine entrance into a reservoir, then through the filters and reverse osmosis purifiers into bottles, crates, and trucks that make deliveries to businesses and homes all over the state. Two hundred and fifty thousand square feet of the mine are curtained off and dehumidified to create a perfect storage area for everything from valuable documents to motor homes. In addition to high security, the mine maintains low light, constant humidity and temperature, no pests, and little chance of damage from natural disasters. Call ahead for a tour at (606) 858–4407. From Nicholasville, go south on Highway 29 about 4 miles, turn left by the sign, and drive down the steep gravel road into the quarry pit. The office is the first building inside the mouth of the mine.

For a dizzying view of High Bridge and the junction of the Kentucky and Dix Rivers, drive another mile south on Highway 29. Notice how the Dix's water is greener than the brown of the Kentucky's. There may also be a thick layer of mist over the Dix due to the fact that the water is released from the bottom of Herrington Lake at Dix Dam.

Lower your canoe from the bluffs by High Bridge and paddle upriver all day. When you reach **Hall's on the River** restaurant (606–527–6620), you'll be hungry enough to finish one of their mouth-watering seafood entrees. Hall's is also famous for take-home foods like beer cheese. If you're a die-hard landlubber, go by road. From Interstate 75, take the Athens-Boonesboro Road exit. From Winchester, take Highway 627 down to the river. On the way down, you may want to veer to the right when the road intersects Old Boonesboro Road and watch for Old Stone Church Road and the lovely little church by the same name. Supposedly the first church established west of the Appalachian Mountains, it still has an active congregation, but they don't mind visitors as long as you don't leave trash.

Though the telephone has radically altered our society and world, it is seldom commemorated. Winchester's Pioneer Telephone Museum is one of a kind. The collection of antique phones, phone booths, switchboards, and other phone memorabilia is housed in the phone company's maintenance building at 203 Forest Avenue. From Winchester, go west on Highway 60 past the cemetery; turn right at the first light onto Forest.

You've probably heard that Indians did not have permanent habitations in Kentucky because it was a commonly owned hunting ground. Not true. Thirty-five-hundred acres in southeastern Clark County were occupied, farmed, kept clear, and hunted on by Shawnee Indians. Archaeologists are in search of the Shawnee village called "Eskippakithiki" or "blue lick place" so-called because of its salt-sulphur springs that attracted game to the area. So, if you happen upon a passel of arrowheads while walking across a plowed field here, call the archaeologists.

If you are driving near the Mount Sterling Plaza on the bypass, stop at Arby's. Don't eat. Just get out of the car and look for a rather abrupt grassy knob. That's the Gaitskill Mound, an Adena burial mound dating from 800 B.C. to A.D. 700.

Although they're not of the same magnitude, this area boasts two other cultural artifacts, instances of a nearly extinct type of American entertainment, the Drive-In Theater. The Sky-Vue Drive-In (606–744–6663) is situated about halfway between Lexington and Winchester near the intersection of Highways 60 and 1678, and the Judy Drive-In (606–498–1960) is north of Mount Sterling in Judy on Highway 11. Both are open from Memorial Day to Labor Day with feature films beginning nightly at sundown.

In downtown Mount Sterling there are yet two more artifacts from the 1950s. Berryman's Tasty Treat, on East Main Street since 1951, is a full-fledged vintage carry-out dairy freeze famous for their chili hotdogs. Dad's Grill at 102 West Main Street is a mere replica, but full-fledged nonetheless. Wayne Welch and Farrell Barnes recently transformed the old diner into what would have been a hip joint in the 1950s. There's a be-bop juke box, spinning stools lined up by a long, shiny counter, eight by ten glossies of James Dean and other period teen idols, old record albums on display, early neon lights, and the smell of french fries in the air. For low prices you can order Coney Islands, Big Bopper Burgers, Malted Shakes, and Cherry Cokes. No item on the menu is more than $2.65. Swell, huh? Hours are 7:30 A.M. to 9:00 P.M., Monday through Thursday, 7:30 A.M. to 11:00 P.M. on Friday and Saturday, and 8:00 A.M. to 9:00 P.M. on Sunday. Call (606) 498–0132.

For more area information, stop by the Chamber of Commerce at 51 North Maysville Street, in the old Bell House building, circa 1815, previously a hat shop and the county jail. Uphill at the corner of Broadway and High streets is the Ascension Episcopal Church, a beautiful little church with walnut paneling, exquisite carved wood, exposed beams, and stained-glass windows thought to be the first to cross the mountains (by oxcart!). The doors are open during the day so visitors can marvel at the 1877 gem.

Around the corner at 321 Maysville Street is the Trimble House Bed and Breakfast, owned by Jim and June Hyska. They have a suite, a small apartment, and several rooms that share baths. Call (606) 498–6561 for reservations. If you're a history buff, make arrangements to tour Morgan Station, the site of the first Indian raid in Kentucky. Daniel Boone's cousin, Ralph Morgan, built the big stone house east of Mount Sterling at 3751 Harpers Ridge Road. The owner, Danny Montgomery, is often willing to show visitors around. Call first at (606) 498–2011.

If you're serious about quilts, make an appointment to see Polly Smith, a nationally acclaimed quilter who does custom work of all kinds, including patchwork, appliqué, and embroidering. She usually has a few exquisite finished quilts on hand for folks who drop by; prices start at $300. Call Polly at (606) 498–0333. Other craftspeople to visit are Doug and Jeannie Naselroad who have been making door harps and custom guitars for more than twenty years. You'll see (and hear) them at most state craft shows. Call ahead (606–498–3724), but you're welcome to visit. From town, take High Street to the bypass and turn on Grassy Lick Road; turn left on Howell-Drennen Road and watch for their sign.

Now for dessert. Make a run to Townsend's Sorghum Mill at 11620 Main Street (also Highway 460) in Jeffersonville, south of Mount Sterling. Go any time of year because they always have pure sorghum syrup (and occasionally maple syrup) on hand. From mid-September through November you can watch them process the cane. Call Judy and Danny Townsend at (606) 498–4142 or plan to come by after 4:00 P.M.

The ultimate dessert is chocolate—real food for real people. Walk into **Ruth Hunt Candies** and faint. The aroma of liquid chocolate, sweet cream, and roasting nuts will seduce even those with great self-restraint. Everything is handmade and very fresh. Just like in the old days, you can ask the clerk for a quarter pound of pulled cream candy, a half pound of caramel and bittersweet chocolate balls, and a handful of hot cinnamon suckers and then watch them reach into the big, colorful bins for the goods.

This operation is small and friendly enough that Larry Kezele, the owner, may have time to show you the whole operation. Ruth Tharpe Hunt started the business in 1921 after her bridge buddies encouraged her to go public with her candy-making. The Blue Monday Sweet Bar, a dark chocolate with pulled cream in the center, perhaps the most famous of their products, was named by a traveling minister who was eating Sunday dinner at the Hunts and claimed that he needed candy to get through those blue Mondays. Look for Larry and his staff dressed like Blue Mondays in parades. The company is located at 426 West Main Street and is open Monday through Thursday from 8:30 A.M. to 5:00 P.M., Friday and Saturday from 9:00 A.M. to 6:00 P.M., and Sunday from 1:00 to 6:00 P.M. Call (606) 498–0676 if you need more information.

City Lights

"When I start working, I might as well climb into the wood—that's how intimate it gets," says woodworker Connie Carlton of Lawrenceburg. Connie looks for the perfect tree in the woods, cuts it before the sap runs, splits long sections of the trunk lengthwise with a sledge and froe, and shapes the wood on a vice-bench of ancient design called a "shaving horse" amidst a tiny sea of curled wood shavings. (The place smells like heaven.) The results are long, smooth, shapely pitchforks, rakes, barrel staves, woodworking tools, and the like. He also makes sorghum and cuts hair. If you want to buy fine wooden tools or get your hair cut by a man with a steady hand, take Highway 127 to Highway 62 west about 2 miles and turn left on Rice Road. His is the first house on the left. Call ahead at (606) 839–6478.

More than 95 percent of the bourbon whiskey made in America is made in Kentucky, and most of it comes from this area. **Wild Turkey Distilleries** (of Boulevard Distillers and Importers, Inc.) is just the place to get a fascinating bourbon education. From Lawrenceburg, take Highway 62 east of town until it splits with Highway 1510. Bear right, go downhill, and watch for the Visitors Information Center on the right. (Note the high train trestle spanning the Kentucky River. Young's High Bridge is a single-span, deck-over cantilever, 281 feet high and 1,659 feet long—the last of its kind.)

The Wild Turkey Distilleries has been operating continuously since the mid-1860s, except during Prohibition when nearly all distilleries were shut down. During World War II this facility made only surgical alcohol. Federal law states that for whiskey to be bourbon, it must be manufactured in the United States of at least 51 percent corn and stored at 125 proof or less for at least two years in new, charred, white oak barrels. Char caramelizes the wood, a process that gives the bourbon its rich color and flavor. At Wild Turkey Distilleries the corn is ground, cooked, and cooled. The distillers add rye for starch, then barley malt, which converts the starch to sugar (moonshiners simply dump cane sugar into the corn mash). Yeast is added, and when the fermented mash is steamed from below, whiskey vapor rises to the top where it is condensed into liquid form. The whiskey is distilled again, put into barrels, and aged for eight years. It's tasted at every stage, and meticulous production records are kept for every batch. Tours are available between 8:30 A.M. and 2:30 P.M. The distillery operates twenty-four hours a day every day except Sunday when liquor is not made anywhere. Call (502) 839–4544.

From Lawrenceburg take Highway 127 north into Frankfort, the state capital. On Second Street look for an ornate Queen Anne-style house with gingerbread trim, the official Visitor Center (502–875–TOUR). Because the city's layout is confusing, a map is as good as a headache prevention pill.

Directly across Capitol Avenue from the Visitors Center is Rebecca-Ruth Candy, Inc. at 112 East Second Street. Chocolate and candy addicts will love the tour of one of Kentucky's oldest houses of sweet repute. In 1919 Rebecca Gooch and Ruth (Hanly) Booe stopped teaching and went into the business of making candy. Ruth's son, John Booe, is the president of the company, and his son, Charles (who claims to eat a pound of candy a day), intends to uphold the tradition.

Tour the production area to see pipes running full of liquid Dutch chocolate and churning vats full of sugar and thick cream. Edna Robbins, expert confectioner of sixty-two years, makes some candies completely by hand on the original 1919 marble slab. Rebecca-Ruth sells literally hundreds of varieties, including delicate mints, crunchy chocolate turtles, fudge galore, and variations on the delicious theme of the bourbon ball. The sales room is tantalizing. For a free catalog call (800) 444–3766. Hours are Monday through Saturday from 8:00 A.M. to 5:30 P.M. Tours of the facility are given Monday through Thursday from January through October. Call (502) 223–7475 for tour schedule.

Downtown on St. Clair Mall, an old street partially sectioned off for pedestrians only, is **Rick's City Café** (502–223–5525), a hoppin' spot in Frankfort. On Thursday nights Rick's offers the only indoor dinner theater in the state. The stage is a small, carpeted platform transformed with great economy by the HAK theater company into a convincing performance area. The plays vary from Christmas traditionals like *The Gift of the Magi* to more experimental one-acts by Harold Pinter and popular new plays like *Greater Tuna*. Wednesday nights are cosmopolitan, truly at the edge of interactive video entertainment. From 8:00 P.M. to midnight Rick's runs a laser video disk machine known as Karaoke Showtime. For a $2 cover charge you can vie for a turn singing a hit song of your choice with the Japanese machine. You're on stage with the mike, and the Karaoke does the rest—lights, back-ups, and music. You take home a free audiocassette of you making a fool of yourself.

Across from Rick's on St. Clair Mall, stop in to Selbert's Jewelry, open since 1872 and barely changed. The ceilings are covered in the original pressed tin, and the wood and glass display cases are in beautiful condition, their curved edges worn soft by more than 119 years of yearning shoppers. Down St. Clair Mall and over the bridge, look for the White Light Diner (502–227–4889), an irresistible little hamburger joint that's been doing regular business since 1927. The signs painted on the wall by the door read Courteous Service and, my favorite, Ladies Invited. Hours are Monday through Saturday, 6:30 A.M. to 2:30 P.M. For the full effect, order the Blue Plate special and sit on one of the spinning stools at the counter.

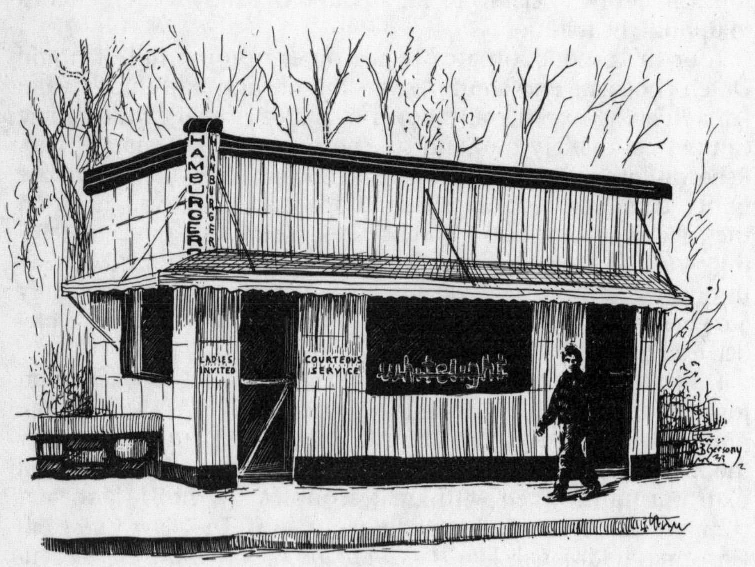

White Light Diner

Another dining establishment with interesting atmosphere is The Cave Restaurant at 100 Workhorse Alley. Caverns were constructed on the site in 1805 for brewing and storing beer. During the Civil War old beer barrels from The Capitol Brewery were piled on the hill behind The Cave to simulate artillery. Supposedly this intimidated Confederate raiders for a time, although the city was eventually taken. During Prohibition the caverns were filled with dirt, but in 1972 Rodney Ratliff hauled the dirt back out of a few front rooms and built a restaurant now open daily for lunch and dinner. Call (502) 875–7119.

Take a ride outside of town to **Luscher's Farm Relics of Yesterday:** Museum of the American Farmer. This unusual museum has the commendable mission of preserving the history of American agriculture, and it does so, in part, by displaying a great deal of old equipment (that works!). From town, take Wilkinson Street east past the Ancient Age Distillery and turn left at the Department of Transportation building onto Lewis Ferry Road. In a couple of miles, bear right onto Manley-Leestown Road and look for the sign.

On display are rows and rows of Luscher family pieces and other collected items that were used in Kentucky from 1840 to the present—Model-T trucks, steel-wheeled tractors, wooden plows, a steam engine, horse-drawn mowing machines, hundreds of smaller tools like wrenches, yokes, ice picks, saws, sickles, churns, washing machines, and so on. The tool with the best story is a 1922 limestone pulverizer. In the words of Albert Luscher, "when it was first used the neighbors remarked about those crazy Luschers, picking up rocks on their fields, grinding them up into dust, and putting them back on the fields. Pretty soon though, everybody was liming their fields." From Memorial Day to Labor Day, hours are 10:00 A.M. to 4:00 P.M. Monday through Saturday, and on Sunday from 1:00 to 4:00 P.M. or by appointment. Call (502) 875–2755.

Go west on Interstate 64 or Highway 60 to Shelbyville. In 1825 Julia Tevis founded **Science Hill,** a girls' school on Washington Street in downtown Shelbyville, because she believed young women needed an education in math and science, not just needlepoint and etiquette. During its 114-year operation Science Hill was known as one of the best preparatory schools in the country. Etiquette, however, never lost its essential place. A former student remembers this story about Miss Julia Poynter, the last principal of the school: The mother of a "town boy" had a party in her home.

One of the students thanked the hostess by saying, "I enjoyed myself thoroughly." Miss Julia reprimanded the girl, saying, "You do not go to a party to enjoy yourself, you go to enjoy others. Tell your hostess that you enjoyed her party."

Today the fully restored Science Hill complex houses six boutiques, the Wakefield-Scearce Galleries, and a restaurant, The Georgia Room of Science Hill Inn. In keeping with the nineteenth-century atmosphere, the restaurant serves fine American food with a heavy Kentucky accent. Lunch is served daily (except Monday) from 11:30 A.M. to 2:30 P.M., and dinner is served 6:00 to 8:00 P.M. Thursday through Saturday. Call (502) 633–2825 for reservations. Wakefield-Scearce Galleries are chock-full of elegant English (plus a touch of Oriental, American, and European) furniture, silver, china, rugs, paintings, and other decorative objects. Much of the furniture is antique, and the reproductions are beautifully made. The quality is high, as are the prices. For example, a fifteen-piece set of English Copeland china with hand-painted Loch scenes, circa 1850, sells for $2,850. Whether or not you can afford to buy, these museumlike galleries provide room after room of visual and tactile delight.

A few blocks west of Wakefield-Scearce on the right side of Washington Street, follow the bagpipe music to Sally and Murray Nicol's store, The Scotland Yard, Kentucky's only all-Scottish extravaganza. There is a chart listing family names and their respective tartan plaids. If your last name is Douglas, Stewart, or, Lord help you, Colquhoun or Farquharson, you will be able to find ties, skirts, and scarves in all possible weave variations on your tartan. All 490 tartans are represented as are family crests, clan car badges, kilt outfits, bagpipe supplies, maps, jewelry, music, and a room full of very British foods. Hours are 10:00 A.M. to 5:00 P.M., except Sunday (502–633–0116).

Park anywhere in downtown Shelbyville and walk to see why Shelbyville considers itself the antique capital of Kentucky. Antiques, specialty gift shops, and galleries line Washington and Main streets as well as all the side streets. If you want to spend the night near town, try the Muir House Bed and Breakfast, located just off Old Taylorsville Road on a lovingly landscaped twelve-acre site overlooking Clear Creek. The house is considered a fine example of the American Shingle Style. Notice the graceful stairway and Palladian arches by the front entrance. Call Steve and Deb Grunst at (502) 633–7037 to reserve any of the three rooms.

In the early nineteenth century when Highway 60 was called "the Lexington and Louisville Turnpike," the Old Stone Inn, circa 1820, was well known as a hospitable stagecoach inn and tavern. New proprietors have restored the inn as a restaurant, gift shop, and bed and breakfast facility. The old dinner bell rings for lunch from 11:00 A.M. to 3:00 P.M., Wednesday through Saturday, and for dinner from 5:30 to 8:00 P.M. on the same days. Sunday brunch is served from 11:00 A.M. to 3:30 P.M. Four rooms on the second floor are used for lodgings at the rate of $75 per night. Call (502) 722–8882 for reservations. Old Stone Inn is 8 miles west of Shelbyville on Highway 60.

In Simpsonville, take Highway 1848 north to the Todds Point Country Store, the hot spot for lunch and local fun. The food is tasty—homemade soups of the day, barbecue, bratwurst, and any type of sandwich you can dream up. Big bowls of unshelled peanuts are on the tables for snacking. The Pinnicks sell groceries, too, and a little hardware, but the greatest allure is the Nerf basketball hoop above the drink cooler: Make one shot in three and you win a free cup of coffee; make two and you also get your choice of doughnut. The stiffest competition comes from a table near the free-throw line with a sign above it reading LIAR'S TABLE. You'll know where to sit.

From Todds Point, take Highway 362 into Peewee Valley. Turn right by the tracks on Highway 393 and go north a block to Barnett's Antiques, a haven for visual grazing (502–241–4277). J. C. Barnett has a fantastic collection of stoneware jugs and crocks. The JUGS WANTED poster hanging by the front door proves that his appetite is not satisfied. Pottery lovers will be taken, heart and soul, by the pieces with so-called defects.

South of Peewee Valley and west of everything else in Central Kentucky is Louisville, largest city in the state and home of the world-famous Kentucky Derby. The greatest two minutes in sports is also part of the greatest twenty-four hours in fashion. For a week before the Derby, everyone and everything is dressed to the nines—houses are repainted, yards are relandscaped, and bodies are clothed in the latest styles, no matter what the cost and no matter what the weather. For Kentuckians, the Derby marks the beginning of early summer and, therefore, the first day that it's okay for women to shed their dark winter garb and wear white again. Fashion sometimes follows need and sometimes it leads. Several years ago we had a bitter cold, rainy Derby Day, but the dresses were purchased and hats were garnished. . . . Women wore thermal underwear under sleeveless gowns and men, for once, were happy to keep on their coats and ties.

The Kentucky Derby is run the first Saturday in May at the Churchill Downs Race Track (502–636–4400) on Central Avenue. The gates open at 8:00 A.M., and you can join the party on the Infield for $20 a head, or you can opt for the classier seats in the Clubhouse Grounds for $30. Racing begins at 11:30 A.M., but the Run for the Roses isn't until 5:30 P.M. Dress however you want and keep your eyes peeled for celebrities. Churchill Downs also hosts thoroughbred racing during a Spring Meet, which runs from the end of April to the beginning of July, and a Fall Meet, which runs from late October through late November.

If you're planning to be seen at the Derby and want to be on the cutting edge of fashion, you might want to check out the annual pre-Derby fashion show held in mid-April at the Kentucky Derby Museum (502–637–1111) on the grounds of Churchill Downs. Celebs and local media personalities model the latest in hats and clothes, setting a precedent for the masses. Any time of year the Derby Museum is an interesting stop. Naturally, many exhibits concentrate on the Derby's history, but others focus on the whole thoroughbred industry. Hours are 9:00 A.M. to 5:00 P.M. daily. Also on site is the Finish Line Gift Shop and The Derby Cafe.

A few miles east of the thoroughbreds, standardbreds race south of Interstate 264 on Poplar Level Road (Highway 864) on the Louisville Downs Race Track, the biggest standardbred track in the state. Their season begins after Christmas and goes until the end of April. Call (502) 964–3616 for specific information.

Far from the madding crowd but not far from Louisville Downs are several peaceful sites. The most surprising is inside the Interstate 264 loop between Poplar Level Road and Newburg Road. Called the Beargrass Creek State Nature Preserve, this forty-one-acre woods has a remarkably diverse community of flora and fauna, and, since it's smack-dab in the middle of the city, it is constantly in use for environmental education. So if you placed all your bets badly at the track, here's a balm. This lovely spot is open daily from sunrise to sunset year-round.

The park is named after Beargrass Creek, which empties into the Ohio River above the famous Falls of the Ohio, a rocky series of rapids over a 3-mile descent. In colonial years Beargrass Creek was often used as a resting spot for southbound travelers who needed to develop a strategy for getting around the falls. George Rogers Clark set up a military and civilian camp on nearby Corn Island in 1778. Floods on the island caused the settlers to move to the mainland (somewhere between what is now Twelfth and Rowan streets) and so start building the city of Louisville. Since the installation of the Portland Canal and the McAlpine Dam (easily seen from town near the Northwestern Parkway and Twenty-seventh Street), the Falls of the Ohio is an exposed coral reef, a fossil bed more than 350 million years old. To get a good look at the fossils, cross the river into Clarksville, Indiana, park at the Riverside Park, and walk to the point that the Fourteenth Street railroad bridge and five dam gates meet the shore.

Next to Beargrass Creek Park is the Louisville Zoological Garden at 100 Trevelian Way. Home to more than 900 animals, the zoo has just opened an exhibit of birds of prey and an HerpAquarium, which features a simulated rain forest. Open daily. Call (502) 459–2181.

From the zoo, take Newburg Road to Eastern Parkway and go west to Third Street; turn right and you're on the University of Louisville campus. The **J. B. Speed Art Museum** (502–636–2893) at 2035 South Third Street is an outstanding museum not to be missed at any cost. The permanent collection comprises works from all periods, including some distinguished Medieval, Renaissance, and Dutch masterpieces, and a broad representation of contemporary art. They also maintain a stimulating schedule of traveling exhibitions. Hours are 10:00 A.M. to 4:00 P.M., Tuesday through Saturday, and Sunday from 1:00 to 5:00 P.M. During the summer more culture is in store at the corner of Fourth and Magnolia streets in Central Park. The Kentucky Shakespeare Festival performs free, high-quality live Shakespeare productions from mid-June to early August. Curtain time is 8:30 P.M.

Indoor theater is always happening in this town. Check the *Louisville Courier Journal* for performances by the small theater companies and check the schedule at Actors Theatre, 316 West Main Street. In addition to producing a surprising variety of plays all year (except during July and August), Actors has become nationally known for the Humana Festival of New American Plays and a festival called Classics in Context. Shows in both festivals are booked early, so make reservations by calling (502) 585–1210. There's a restaurant downstairs at Actors.

Main Street is art street. The glass structure with the big whimsical sculpture is the Kentucky Center for the Arts at 609 West Main Street. It hosts a little of everything, including the Louisville Opera, ballet, orchestra, theater for all ages, and a series of national and regional performers. Call (502) 584–7777. A few doors down, the Kentucky Art and Craft Gallery (502–589–0102) features the work of some of the state's finest craftspeople. Nearby is the Zephyr Gallery, an art cooperative that never fails to hang imaginative shows. The last stop is perfect for kids. The Museum of History and Science (502–561–6100) is a big, colorful, hands-on place orchestrated for discovery. The selling point for adults is the IMAX theater, a four-story screen surrounded by speakers; the experience blows your confidence in logic to pieces. "It's just a movie," you tell yourself as you clutch the sides of your seat to keep from falling. Check the museum for showtimes.

Louisville is a big city with almost endless places to explore, but you're likely to miss the following quirky spots. Stay and dig around awhile. If you plan to spend the night, one source of current information about interesting places of lodging is the Kentucky Homes Bed & Breakfast (502–635–7341) at 1431 Saint James Court. One place near the downtown area is The Victorian Secret at 1132 South First Street. Another possibility is the Old Louisville Inn Bed & Breakfast at 1359 South Third Street, a grand eleven-room inn that serves fresh bread for breakfast. Call (502) 635–1574 for reservations.

If you are out on the town late at night and have a hankering for a bite to eat, I can recommend no more colorful place than Irma's Cafe, a twenty-four-hour soul food emporium. Breakfast is served anytime and the steamtable is always full of such delectables as fried apples, spicy sweet potatoes, corn on the cob, mashed potatoes and gravy, corn fritters, and a meat or two. Irma's is on the corner of Broadway and Twenty-sixth Street. Call (502) 776–9576 or 776–9261.

Since so many restaurants of every kind are in town, let's consider dessert. The prize for the most unusual business combination that serves dessert is the Quonset Hut Concrete Statuary Garden and Ice Cream at the Overlook (502–584–0814). You can eat ice cream or frozen yogurt while you shop for concrete bird baths, statues, pots, urns, or garden fountains, all at reasonable prices. Or you can simply gaze down from the top of Phoenix Hill onto the Louisville skyline. This is a good place for a first date. Take Broadway west to Baxter Avenue and turn left; turn left again up Hull Street, and you're there. Hours are 4:00 to 10:00 P.M. Monday through Friday, 9:00 A.M. to 10:00 P.M. on Saturday, and 1:00 to 10:00 P.M. on Sunday.

Kizito Cookies (502–456–2891) wins a prize for the most unusual method of dessert distribution. During lunch hours the owner, Elizabeth Kizito, carries a basket of scrumptious chocolate chip cookies through the downtown streets *on her head.* She is from Uganda, where it's commonplace for folks to keep their hands free by means of this balancing act, but in Louisville, she's become famous for it. These days she has a retail store, also called Kizito Cookies, at 1398 Bardstown Road where you can buy coffee, cookies, and muffins while looking over a colorful selection of African earrings, hats, and clothing. Hours are Tuesday through Friday, 7:00 A.M. to 6:00 P.M., and Saturday, 9:00 A.M. to 6:00 P.M.

More wonderful African-oriented arts are displayed at **Kente International** (502–459–4594) at 1954 Bonnycastle Avenue. The gallery/store carries a line of imported goods from South America, Pakistan, India, and Africa. You'll fall in love with the colorful clothing and tapestries and the striking jewelry and sculpture. The owner, Musa Uthman, is a percussionist extraordinaire and, not surprisingly, sells handmade drums from Africa and India; he also carries a few made by Native Americans. The most popular is the beautiful Djamba drum from Senegal; hand-carved from a hard, local wood, it has a goatskin head that is tuned with ropes. Musa teaches basic techniques and rhythms during drum workshops he gives by appointment on Sundays and after hours. The store is open from 10:30 A.M. to 7:30 P.M. Monday through Saturday.

Two well established potteries can be found in Louisville, and both are worth a visit. Louisville Stoneware, famous for dinnerware, is really a pottery industry, but the process is almost the same as you would find in the small studio of an individual potter. They're located at 731 Brent Street. Tours are available twice a day, and pottery is offered for sale in a retail showroom (502–582–1900). Hadley Pottery (502–584–2171) in Butchertown at 1570 Storey Avenue was started by Mary Hadley in 1940. Her original style has been maintained and although the pieces are no longer hand-thrown, they are all hand-painted. Come at 2:00 P.M. for a guided tour. Showroom hours are 8:30 A.M. to 4:30 P.M. Monday through Friday, and 9:00 A.M. to 12:30 P.M. on Saturday.

If you're looking for antique pottery and almost anything else imaginable, pay a visit to **Joe Ley Antiques, Inc.** at 615 East Market Street. Joe Ley's place is two acres under one roof and full—I mean *full*—of antique treasures. For architects and home restoration folks, this is an endless toy shop. Stained glass, chandeliers, mantels, carousel horses, stuffed moose, fine silver—you name it, it's here. Hours are Tuesday through Saturday, 8:00 A.M. to 5:00 P.M. Call (502) 583–4014.

Antiques of an aural sort are found at an obscure little record store downtown at 240 West Jefferson, between Second and Third Streets. Called King's Records, the place was more obscure before Rosanne Cash, country music singer and daughter of Johnny Cash, entitled a recent album "King's Records," the cover of which had a picture of Rosanne leaning against King's door. To tell the truth, Rosanne's image was superimposed on a photograph taken by Hank DeVito, her guitarist, when he was in town with another band. Owner Gene King's big brothers are Country Music Hall of Famer Pee Wee King, who wrote "The Tennessee Waltz," Tennessee's state song, with Redd Steward in 1947, and Max King, who's in the Jazz Hall of Fame. Gene, a music connoisseur, has developed a record collection that draws customers from around the globe. His expertise is in country music, but you can find a little bit of everything at King's, and, as a bonus, you get a story about whatever you purchase. Hours are Monday through Saturday, 10:00 A.M. to 5:00 or 6:00 P.M. Call (502) 584–5535.

Another little-known cultural reference library of sorts is found in the halls of Tattoo Charlie's, a dermagraphic extravaganza. Tattoo art has come a long way since bones and charcoal or needles in a cork. For the uninitiated, you can watch consenting clients being decorated by a certified tattoo technician wielding an electric needle that looks and sounds like a dentist's drill. Prices range from $25 for a single music note, for example, to more than $3,000 for a series of full-color illustrations. Even if you aren't personally interested in a tattoo, check out the tattoo design gallery. Owner and tattoo master Charlie Wheeler has lined the walls with possible patterns. Charlie has also posted hundreds of photographs and slides of customers displaying actual tattoos, no matter where they are. Charlie has a motorcycle seat in his booth where you can relax and watch the show or, perhaps, try out your new tattoo in the correct posture. Tattoo Charlie's is located at 1845 Berry Boulevard, on the south side of town; the easiest way to get threre is to take

Highway 31 south and turn east on Seventh Street Road, then veer onto Berry Boulevard. No appointment necessary. Call (502) 366–9635 for hours.

Now, to escape the city's rush, take Bardstown Road east until it splits with Taylorsville Road (Highway 155) and follow the latter 1 mile east of Jeffersontown. Before you cross the Gene Snyder Freeway, look for Tucker Station Road on the left (north) and follow signs to Blackacre State Nature Preserve, part of the Tyler Settlement Rural Historic Preserve. Blackacre is used for environmental and agricultural education of schoolchildren and visitors of all ages. The idea is to foster a sense of stewardship for the land. A working farm on the preserve is farmed according to ecologically sound practices—the land is plowed and hayed with draft horses, and gardens are raised organically. Groups meet and have programs here, but Blackacre is open to other visitors also. You'll find the clear thinking and the beautiful environment refreshing in deep ways. The experience will make you want to hurry home to your own garden. To arrange a visit, call Project I.D. at (502) 473–3295.

Abbeys and Art

What was once an abused tract of tired farmland is now **Bernheim Forest** Arboretum and Nature Center, a 10,000-acre native forest protected since 1928. Available in this legacy of the "Knobs" are hiking, picnicking, limited fishing, unlimited daydreaming, and a self-education in the Nature Center's museum or in the arboretum, where an enormous variety of ornamental plants are grown in meticulously labeled manicured beds. I used to skip high school in the spring to make an annual pilgrimage here armed with my bicycle and a sketch pad. The forest is open from March 15 to November 15, daily from 9:00 A.M. to 6:00 P.M. No groups of more than twenty people are allowed in the forest at a time. Call (502) 543–2451 for information. Bernheim Forest is next to the intersection of Interstate 65 (Exit 112) and Highway 245.

While traveling, Mark Twain was asked by the luggage inspector if he had anything besides clothing in his suitcase. Twain said "No," but I guess he looked suspicious because the man opened his case anyhow and found a fifth of bourbon whiskey. "I thought you had only clothes!" the man roared. "Ahh," Twain answered, "but that's my nightcap." Twain's drink of choice had to be bourbon, and it had to be from the limestone hills of Kentucky that provide the water that gives Jim Beam and other regional bourbons a distinctive flavor that makes them the best in the world. For a crash course in whiskey mash, take a free tour of the Jim Beam American Outpost and museum (502–543–9877) on Highway 245, a mile east of Bernheim Forest. Hours are 9:00 A.M. to 4:30 P.M., Monday through Saturday, and 1:00 to 4:00 P.M. on Sunday.

If you're going toward Bardstown from the west on Highway 245, not stopping at Rooster Run General Store is like being in Memphis and skipping Graceland. The store, formerly called Evans Beverage Depot, was the only place in Nelson County in the late sixties that sold alcohol. One day a man had too many drinks, and his wife showed up with fire in her eyes, stood in the door, and snarled his name. When the drunk man sped to her side, someone remarked, "Well would you look at that old rooster run." Such is the history of town names in our state. I still wonder whether the fact that the next town over is called Hen Peck had anything to do with the previous story. Whatever the truth may be, Joe Evans put the place on the map by selling more than a million Rooster Run caps to truck drivers and celebrities alike.

Bardstown is dense with well advertised, historically significant treasures, like My Old Kentucky Home State Park and the house of John Rowan. Rowan invited his Pittsburgh cousin, Stephen Foster, to visit in 1852, and shortly afterwards, Foster wrote the tune that is now our official state song. The mansion and gardens are open year round. From June 9 to September 2 the famous musical, "The Stephen Foster Story," is performed outdoors. You can't miss the signs.

Most people know about Wickland, the finest example of Georgian architecture in the country and "the only home in America where three governors have lived." Charles Wickliffe, a rags-to-riches figure, built the place in 1815 for his bride, Margaret Crepps. Charles was a Kentucky governor, and his son, Robert, became Louisana's last pre–Civil War governor. Charles and Margaret's daughter, Julia, married William Beckham and had ten children, one, John Crepps Wickliffe Beckham, who also became governor of Kentucky. When the Civil War broke out, the Beckhams were harrassed for their lavish lifestyle and slave ownership, so they fled Wickland for Canada.

As is true for many women during many eras, Julia left behind her record of the times in the form of a quilt. Her stunning, full-sized Baby Blocks quilt is made entirely of silk and velvet pieces from family ball dresses and gowns. Not designed for wear-and-tear, the quilt shows that even after the "recent unpleasantness," Julia had a place in her life for nonfunctional beauty, but also that ball dresses weren't needed any more—posh days were over. Today Wickland's fourteen rooms are fully furnished with exquisite antiques. The museum offers guided tours year-round from 9:00 A.M. to sundown, except on Sundays when it opens at noon. Admission is $3. Go about 1 mile east of Courthouse Square on Highway 62. For more information, write Wickland, P.O. Box 314, Bardstown, KY 40004.

Another old Southern-style mansion that bore big-time political figures into the world is The Mansion at 1003 North Third Street. Now a three-room bed and breakfast, it too is full of period antiques, the most wonderful of which is outside in the yard—Kentucky's second-largest American Elm tree. Daily tours at 5:30 and 6:30 P.M., or by appointment. Call Mr. or Mrs. Joseph Dennis Downs for lodging reservations at (502) 348–2586.

Two on-the-beaten-path restaurants in town are Old Talbott Tavern, the oldest western stagecoach stop in America, circa 1779, which also has bed and breakfast lodging in the old inn (502–348–3494) and My Old Kentucky Dinner Train (502–348–7500), where you dine in vintage 1940s dining cars pulled by old diesel electric engines on a two-hour ride to Limestone Springs and back. Both have their merits, but *the* local place to eat is the Hurst Restaurant, a small downtown diner facing the Courthouse Square. The soups are homemade, and the local talk is always juicy.

While you're downtown in Courthouse Square, pay your respects to John Fitch, the unhappy inventor of the steamboat in 1791. Then listen to the earth rumble when Robert Fulton turns over in his grave—wherever he's buried, may he rest in some peace. John Fitch was not born in Bardstown, but he died here after a lifetime of work on steam navigation and a lifetime of struggle with inventor James Rumsey, who, like Fulton, claimed to have been the first to apply it successfully. After failing to get sponsors, analogous to today's lusted-after research grants, Fitch came to Nelson County, built steamboat models, and tested them in local streams. Fitch's grave in the square is marked by a small steamboat replica.

At the corner of Highway 62 West (also called Stephen Foster Avenue) and Fifth Street are the Saint Joseph Proto-Cathedral and Spalding Hall. The cathedral, circa 1823, is the oldest cathedral west of the Alleghenies and contains a collection of paintings given by the French king Louis Phillippe, Francis I, king of the Two Sicilies, and Pope Leo XII. Six solid tree trunks, lathed and plastered, were transformed into the building's huge Corinthian columns. St. Joseph's is open daily. Call (502) 348–3126.

Behind the cathedral is Spalding Hall, circa 1826, a large brick building that was originally part of Saint Joseph College, Seminary, and later Prep School. Two adjoining museums here are the Bardstown Historical Museum and the Oscar Getz Museum of Whiskey History, both free. Displays range from items like Jenny Lind's cape and Jesse James's hat to an original 1854 E. G. Booz bottle, which inspired the word "booze," and a Carrie Nation exhibit. Hours from May through October are Monday to Saturday, 9:00 A.M. to 5:00 P.M., and Sunday 1:00 to 5:00 P.M. From November through April, they open at 10:00 A.M. and close at 4:00 P.M., except on Sundays when they open at 1:00 P.M. Downstairs, La Taberna Restaurant and Lounge is a classy place to eat lunch or dinner seven days a week any time between 11:00 A.M. and 1:00 A.M.

Think about the basis of homesteading—self-sufficiency. Now apply the concept to the visual arts, and you will begin to appreciate Jim and Jeannette Cantrell. The Bardstown Art Gallery, downstairs in Spalding Hall, is a fine-art gallery, a framing shop, pottery and painting studios, a printing shop, an office, a home, and a small book sales business that boasts one of the country's most comprehensive collections of Thomas Merton's writings. The Cantrells' love of high quality is apparent in everything from Jim's treatment of light and reflections in his oils to Jeannette's hand-set letterpress gallery announcements. Jeannette arranges group and solo shows in addition to displaying Jim's prints and originals in oil, watercolor, pen and ink, and anything else that caught his eclectic eye. Beware: You'll be tempted to take something home.

It was by accident that Jeannette became a Merton expert. One of the monks at the Abbey of Gethsemani asked if she wouldn't mind selling a few of Merton's books to tourists. She started with a few copies of *Seven Storey Mountain* and now carries a respectable line of Merton's out-of-print writings, valuable limited editions, related scholarly works, and cassettes of Merton himself reading from his works or talking about subjects like Rilke's poetry, silence, art, and beauty. Hours at the Bardstown Art Gallery are officially BY CHANCE OR BY APPOINTMENT, but someone is usually there from 10:00 A.M. to 5:00 P.M., Monday through Saturday, and from 1:00 to 5:00 P.M. on Sunday. Call them at (502) 348–6488.

To visit Thomas Merton's residence, the **Abbey of Gethsemani,** the oldest Cistercian monastery in the New World, follow Highway 31E south from Bardstown, veer left at Culvertown onto Highway 247 and watch for TRAPPISTS signs.

From the heart of Italy around A.D. 500, Saint Benedict developed a set of rules to help monks in a spiritually based community follow the example of Christ as closely as possible. These Trappist monks take vows to renounce the capacity to acquire and possess goods, to obey the house rules and the Abbot's advice, and to remain celibate. Silence is encouraged but not required. "Enclosure," I've been told, "is enforced not so much to

Abbey of Gethsemani

keep lay people out as to keep the monks in." But these monks do indulge in some wandering. Thomas Merton, quintessential ascetic aesthetic monk from this abbey, was known to go "out" to lecture, to meet with other spiritual people, and occasionally to hear jazz in nightclubs. While visiting the abbey, I met a monk who travels to Owensboro for the barbeque festival. And the organist and composer, Brother Chrysogonos, one of this community's two hermits, is a musical genius and often travels to Europe for research. No matter what else you think, their life choice is radical.

Economic survival is perhaps the greatest difference between early and modern cloisters. The seventy-six monks in residence today make and sell fruit cakes and three kinds of Port Salut Trappist cheese, a pungent, creamy, French-style aged cheese. Everyone takes part in all aspects of the work, from making cheese (or packaging imported cheeses) to doing dishes to answering the phone or laying sewer pipes on the 2,000-acre farm.

Lay people are welcome to join in parts of life at the Abbey. Visitors are welcome at Mass, if you can make it at 6:15 A.M. on weekdays (the monks will have been awake for three hours by then!). Sunday Mass is at 10:20 A.M. in the main chapel, a long, narrow, modern building where the choir's chant reverberates as if produced in outer space. Gethsemani has a retreat house with thirty rooms that can be reserved for personal or group retreats. Women are welcome only during the first full week of each month, and men can make retreats anytime. Call far in advance at (502) 549–3117. On the last Sunday of the month at 4:00 P.M., a witty, bright-eyed monk named Brother Paul leads open discussions on Merton's writings. For more information or to order cheese, write Abbey of Gethsemani, Trappist, KY 40051.

One mile south of Gethsemani off Highway 52, with which Highway 247 merges, is the Bethany Spring Retreat House. In 1978 the Sisters of Charity of Nazareth renovated the big farmhouse and opened it as a progressive place of retreat for men and women of all faiths. Up to eight guests at a time can make retreats for $30 a day per person, or $35 if the director, Danielle Witt, acts as spiritual guide. Costs include room and meals. Contact Danielle Witt, SSND, 115 Dee Head Road, New Haven, KY 40051. You can also call (502) 544–8277.

If you drive south from Bardstown and go east at Culvertown (toward Gethsemani), you will arrive in the tiny town of New

Haven. Downtown on Main Street the old train depot now houses the recently reestablished **Kentucky Railway Museum,** where you can hop a train to Boston (that's *Bawston,* Kentucky), 11 miles away on the old Louisville and Nashville Railroad's former Lebanon Branch. Members of the museum completely restored an L & N steam locomotive (No. 152) and the streamlined No. 32 of the former Monon, made in the late 1940s. When these babies pump by, you feel your heart making reply. From May through November, trips run between 10:00 A.M. and 4:00 P.M. on weekends, when the museum and gift shop are also open. June through August it's open daily, except Monday. Fares are $10 for adults, $9 for seniors, and $7 for children aged three to twelve. For exact times and dates write to The Kentucky Railway Museum, P.O. Box 240, New Haven, KY 40051–0240, or call (502) 549–5471 or (800) 272–0152.

To visit one of the state's most famous and picturesque whiskey distilleries, take Highway 52 east from New Haven, or Highway 49 south from Bardstown to Loretto; then take Highway 52 east until you see the sign on the left for Maker's Mark. Like the process, the facility is old. In 1953 Bill Samuels, Sr. bought the shabby country distillery where folks were accustomed to filling their own jugs straight from casks of whiskey in the Quart House. Now Maker's Mark is known around the world for its super-smooth bourbon, nicknamed "Kentucky champagne." The distillery is open daily year-round, except for Saturdays in January and February. Free forty-minute tours are given between 10:30 A.M. and 3:30 P.M., Monday through Saturday. For more information, call (502) 865–2881.

In Loretto, take Highway 49 north, then veer right at a fork in the road onto Highway 152. You'll soon see the sign for Loretto Motherhouse. The Order of the Sisters of Loretto, founded in central Kentucky in 1812, was one of the first American religious communities of women. They moved here in 1824 from Little Loretto at nearby St. Charles. Near the entrance of the grounds is the restored cabin, circa 1808, of Father Charles Nerinckx, founder of the order. Going toward the cemetery, you'll see one of the country's first outdoor Stations of the Seven Dolors, installed in 1911. On the east side of the drive you'll see Knobs Haven, a retreat center where folks can reserve space ($25 for the first day and $20 for each subsequent day) in private or shared rooms. Guests have access to a library, prayer room, and the grounds—three lakes, acres of farmland, wooded areas, and a fitness trail—and can have meals with the whole community in the dining room. Retreatants can engage a Loretto staff member to facilitate conferences or give dream consultation from a Jungian perspective. Contact Elain Prevallet, S.L., Director, Knobs Haven, Nerinx, KY 40049, or call (502) 865–2621.

Next to Loretto's main church and convent, circa 1860–63, you'll notice a group of abstract sculptures in various media. This is the work of Jeanne Dueber, S.L. Her studio is in **Rhodes Hall Art Gallery,** at the north end of the driveway. Her work is amazing in its variety and feeling, and her exploration of form is almost religious. Large refined abstract sculptures in wood, resin, metal, and paper fill the big rooms. A large willow, struck by lightning, has been transformed into a powerful piece called "Tempest," in which Dueber strategically added heads and arms of a man and a woman in such a way that they seem to be sliding away from one another while reaching toward each other. Many pieces are playful and more secular in nature, others are overtly religious. If she's working in the first floor studio and isn't too busy, tell her what you think. The gallery is unlocked daily from 9:00 A.M. to 5:00 P.M. To buy a piece, just put your money in the slotted box by the stairs—a self-service fine-art gallery! Contact Jeanne Dueber, Rhodes Hall, Nerinx, KY 40049, or call (502) 865–5811.

A more secular retreat is to be found at the Blue Hill Farm Bed and Breakfast in Raywick, south of Loretto near the intersection of Highways 528 and 84. Contact Martha and Chet Cramer to stay in their restored two-story log home, circa 1790. For $55 to $65 per night, you get total peace and quiet, pleasant rooms, and breakfast. Martha makes lovely baskets, and Chet is a skilled wood turner. Write to Route #2, Box 39A, Raywick, KY 40060, or call (502) 465–4221.

Go to the center of Lebanon if you want a luxurious meal. Drop your linen napkin on the table and polish off your after-dinner liqueur, and after the waiter sweeps away the clutter of crystal, silver, and painted porcelain, he will offer you a cigar. You will feel like a very special guest indeed at **David's Restaurant** in downtown Lebanon at the corner of Main and Spalding streets. Open for dinner only, nightly from 5:00 to 9:00 P.M., David's serves what owners Stan and Sandy Katz call "hardy European cuisine." The prices range from $6.95 to $14.95 for pasta, steak, and house specialties like beef bourguignonne, and the bar serves a surprising

Rhodes Hall Art Gallery

range of beer, wine, and special drinks. Places like this are real finds anywhere, much less in a one-horse town. Call (502) 692–6874 for reservations.

A few blocks away at 370 North Spalding Street is Myrtledene Bed and Breakfast. The house is an 1833 formal brick affair with a colonial columned portico. The famous Confederate raider General John Hunt Morgan used Myrtledene for headquarters in 1862, and a year later, when he returned with the intention of destroying Lebanon, it was from here that he waved the white flag of surrender. A room and full breakfast are $60 a night. Call (502) 692–2223 for reservations.

Although there were once more than 400 covered bridges in Kentucky, only a handful are left. The Mount Zion Bridge in the northwest corner of Washington County is the only one in this region. Also the only two-span Burr Arch and the longest covered bridge in the state, it was almost lost recently before the county restabilized its piers. It may yet be moved to a more accessible location. For now, the easiest way to see it is to get off the Bluegrass Parkway at Exit 34 and go south on Highway 55; at Mooresville take Highway 458 north and watch for the bridge on the left, spanning the Beech Fork Creek.

Get back to Highway 55 and go north less than a mile; turn south on Highway 529 and bear left at the next **T** in the road. The Glenmar Bed and Breakfast is just outside Fredericktown at the intersection of Grundy Home and Valley Hill roads. This vintage 1785 brick country home is about as cozy a mansion as one could hope for. It has twenty rooms, six bathrooms, and eight fireplaces (Tolstoy would be right at home). Guests can look forward to butterscotch brownies and a hearty country breakfast in the morning. Write to The Glenmar, Route 1, Box 682, Springfield, KY 40069, or call (606) 284–7791.

Like nearby Hodgenville, central Washington County is a repository of sites and stories connected to Abraham Lincoln. Abe's parents, Thomas Lincoln and Nancy Hanks, were from this area, and several of their family buildings are restored or replicated. For details, go by the Lincoln Homestead State Park at the intersection of Highways 438 and 528, 5 miles north of Springfield off Highway 150. An eighteen-hole golf course has been built on old Mordecai Lincoln's land, and I'll bet he's rolling over violently in his grave. The park also has several log structures, including the original Berry Home where Nancy Hanks lived when she and Thomas were courting. The park is open May to September, 8:00 A.M. to 6:00 P.M., and on weekends in October. Ask at the park for a map of the "Lincoln Heritage Trail." For more information, call (606) 336–7461.

In downtown Springfield, notice the Washington County Courthouse on Main Street. Built in 1816, it is the oldest courthouse still in use in Kentucky. Records in the files date back to 1792 and include the marriage certificate of Abraham Lincoln's parents. If court isn't in session, look at copies of this and other documents hanging on the walls. The courthouse is open Monday through Friday, 8:30 A.M. to 4:30 P.M., or Saturday from 9:00 A.M. to noon. Call (606) 336–3471.

The Home Hearth Restaurant near the courthouse is the quintessential local café—steam tables are full of hot "country cooking" and homemade desserts, and the local talk never stops. Before some of us have even reached REM sleep, Brenda Mattingly gets up to make breakfast and cobbler for the day. Hours are 5:30 A.M. to 2:00 P.M. on Monday through Saturday, and 6:30 A.M. to 1:30 P.M. on Sunday. Call (606) 336–7975.

The Maple Hill Manor Bed and Breakfast and gift shop is 2½ miles out of town to the east on Highway 150 (Perryville Road). The house is a striking antebellum Greek Revival mansion, circa 1851. Bob and Kay Carroll have kept this place as fancy as it ought to be and added more than the usual trappings for guests, like a Jacuzzi in the honeymoon room and grills on the patio. Call (606) 336–3075 for reservations.

Off the Beaten Path in Eastern Kentucky

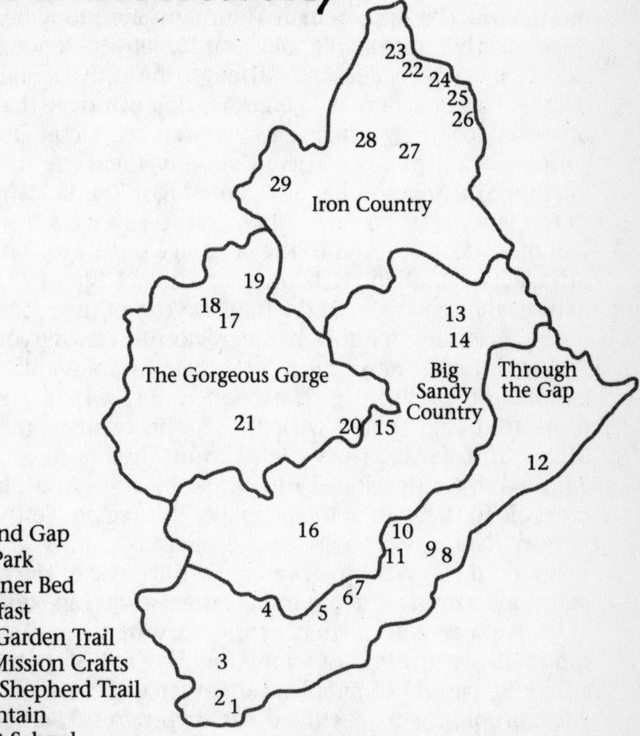

1. Cumberland Gap National Park
2. Ridge Runner Bed and Breakfast
3. Hemlock Garden Trail
4. Red Bird Mission Crafts
5. The Little Shepherd Trail
6. Pine Mountain Settlement School
7. Kingdom Come State Park
8. Bad Branch Nature Preserve
9. Appalshop
10. C. B. Caudill Store
11. Lilley Cornett Woods
12. Breaks Interstate Park
13. Butcher Hollow
14. Jenny Wiley State Resort Park
15. Quicksand Craft Center
16. Frontier Nursing Services
17. Natural Bridge State Resort Park
18. Miguel's Pizza
19. Swamp Valley Store and Museum
20. Robinson Forest
21. Pioneer Museum
22. Jesse Stuart State Nature Preserve
23. Bennett's Mill Bridge
24. Albert's
25. Kentucky Highlands Museum
26. The Piedmont Arts Center
27. Mount Savage Furnace
28. Carter Caves State Resort Park
29. Morehead State University Folk Art Collection

Eastern Kentucky

Most of North America is inhabited by a wild soup of dissenters' descendents, but what makes eastern Kentucky different is the mountains. The Appalachian Mountains are a long beautiful line of steep, nearly impregnable rock that has always tended to keep outsiders out and insiders in. Although the Appalachian culture initially strikes outsiders as foreign, visiting can have the strong allure of a homecoming, in part because your roots may be in European cultures better preserved here than anywhere else in the big melting pot. The isolation has also caused East Kentuckians to live close to the land, close to each other, and to survive self-sufficiently. As you meet people, listen to the language of this region; its beautiful phrases are loaded with humor, knowledge of quirky human nature, and sensitivity to the fragile cycles of the natural world.

Opportunities abound in this region to expose yourself to very fine traditional craftsmanship by meeting individual artists/craftspeople and by visiting craft cooperatives where knowledge and tools are being shared with those who want to take the baton. Music and dance, for which mountaineers have always been admired, have developed in fascinating ways and play an important role in the lives of the people of this region. Festivals and community dances, which are always open to visitors, are good events to attend if you want to get an authentic taste of the music here. In addition to music, the mountains themselves can soothe the soul.

I have a wonderful recent memory of traveling through the mountains at the end of a long, hot day and stopping on a bridge where a "passel" of people had gathered. Below, by the side of a wide brook, a small revival was in progress. Babies were being passed from lap to lap, and people of all ages were sitting in folding chairs by the little stage, clapping and singing. A sweet hymn in an irresistible minor key rising just above the constant tumble of the water calmed me and opened my eyes to the changing mountains, rosy in the last light of the setting sun. Even in the heat of summer, a mist gathers in the folds and hollows of the land and baptizes everyone equally, even passersby.

Through the Gap

Dr. Thomas Walker was hired by Virginia's Loyal Land Company to go west in search of fertile settling land. In 1750 when Walker found the only natural route west, a divide he named Cumberland Gap, he built a small cabin to claim the territory, mapped the route, and went home. You can visit a replica of Walker's crude cabin at the Dr. Thomas Walker State Shrine (606–546–4400) on Highway 459 off Highway 25E southeast of Barbourville. Though they missed reaching the bluegrass region by just a few days of traveling, they succeeded in blazing a trail through the mountains for over 300,000 pioneers to roll toward a new life in the West.

Now Highway 25E cuts through the 20,000-acre **Cumberland Gap National Park.** Go up to the Pinnacle Overlook from which, on those rare clear days, you can see the construction of a tunnel that will go 4,100 feet through the mountain to connect Interstate 75 at Corbin to Interstate 81 at White Pine, Tennessee. The original Cumberland Gap trail will be restored to its 1790–1800 appearance, the way Daniel Boone cut it under the auspices of the Transylvania Company, a broad dirt and rock trail, passable, but not at 65 mph.

More than 50 miles of trails are in the park. One of the most interesting is the Ridge Trail on Brush Mountain, which leads to the Hensley Settlement, a restored cluster of farms and houses inhabited from 1903 until 1951. To drive, take Brownies Creek Road from Cubbage, or take a shuttle from the Visitors' Center in Middlesborough. For all park information, stop by the center during business hours or call (606) 248–2817.

Middlesborough is just north of the gap, outside the National Park, in a circular basin that was probably formed between 30 million and 300 million years ago by a large meteor that disintegrated or was blown back into space upon impact. It is also possible that the basin was formed by the collapse of an underground cavern, since no meteor fragments have been found. Coal, on the other hand, can be found everywhere and is at the heart of the recent history of the area. The Bell County Chamber of Commerce on North 20th Street is housed in a building faced with forty tons of bituminous coal. Next door is The Coal House Museum, a little open-air collection of mining artifacts—old mine train cars, headlamps, drill bits, and photos. Ask about the Cumberland Mountain Fall Festival, held annually in Middlesborough during late October as a celebration of the area's English heritage. The event that will knock your socks off is the Official Kentucky State Banjo Playing Championship. Call (606) 248–1075 for more information.

Follow North Twentieth Street to the top of the hill, turn left on Edgewood, right onto Arthur Heights, and left when the road comes to the edge of the cliff. The second house on the left is the **Ridge Runner Bed and Breakfast,** a grand, twenty-room Victorian-style home built in the early 1890s; it has six rooms available for $35 to $45 per night. A recent tornado narrowly missed the house but managed to clear the trees from the front hillside, leaving an open view of town below. The two women who own and run the place are involved in a fascinating community center/clinic/mission in Stinking Creek, Knox County. Ask them about the history of the center and their continuing work there—great stories. Call (606) 248–4299 for reservations.

Miracle Mountain Crafts is an education and a delight. Go north of Middlesborough about 5 miles on Highway 25E; just north of a bridge and just south of the road's junction with Highway 188 is a small house on the right with a sign in front. James Miracle (pronounced MY-ra-cle) is in his wood shop all day, every day but Sunday. He loves his work, and he'll take time to talk. Since 1967 James has been busy making expressive wooden animals, chairs, and a myriad of toys, the most popular of which is the "limberjack," a jointed puppet that dances when you bounce it on a thin board tucked under your leg. Split oak for chair bottoms, yellow poplar for small animals—all comes from his farm. When an out-of-state customer called to order the biggest dough bowl James could make, he cranked out a massive 28-by-43-by-10-inch yellow poplar bowl, big enough to satisfy even amazon bakers. To place an order, write to James Miracle, Route 2, Box 151, Middlesborough, KY 40965. To visit, call (606) 248–2971, or just surprise him.

Between Middlesborough and Pineville are the Kentucky Ridge State Forest and the Pine Mountain State Resort Pike, both of which have entrances off Highway 25E. Follow signs to the Herndon J. Evans Lodge at the top of the mountain where you can get trail maps and park information, or call (606) 337–3066. At the park's nature center, notice what looks like a petrified tree trunk by the entrance. The trunk was found at a strip mine in northwest Bell county. The tree, which may be 300 million years old, grew in a swampy area and was buried in flood sediments that caused it to rot. Over the course of a few million years, sand percolated through the cavity and hardened, making a fossilized sandstone cast of the tree.

One of the most special trails in the whole state park system is the **Hemlock Garden Trail** through a 782-acre area protected by the Nature Preserves system. The Hemlock Garden is a ravine featuring massive hemlocks, tulip poplars, beech trees, and a beautiful mountain brook. On the southwestern boundary of the park, it can be reached on the Laurel Cove or the Rock Hotel trails. Linger as long as you are able. After all, how often are you in the presence of living beings more than 200 years old?

During the last weekend in May the Mountain Laurel Festival is held to celebrate the blooming of the much-loved mountain flower. The whole event is held in the Laurel Cove Amphitheatre, a beautiful natural stage seating 3,000-plus people, and culminates in the crowning of a Mountain Laurel Queen. The Great American Dulcimer Festival is also held outdoors during the third or fourth weekend of September. This is a wonderful, small festival during which dulcimer makers sell, demonstrate, and teach in booths during the day. At night spectators wrap up in quilts under the stars and watch some of the best performers play on a stage behind a reflective pond. Styles range from traditional folks like Jean Ritchie to classical, pop, big band, and country rock-style players, all on lap or hammered dulcimers.

From within Pine Mountain State Park, go west on Highway 190 toward Frakes. Along the way, in Chenoa, stop by Kathy's Needle and Thread to see traditional quilting in action. The large quilting frames hang from the ceiling in the old way and are lowered to chair height for work. Most work is commissioned, but finished pieces are always available for sale. If you have a quilt-top tucked away in the attic and would like to sleep under it, contact Kathy at (606) 337–6753. Hours are Monday through Friday from 8:00 A.M. to 6:00 P.M. Write Kathy's Needle and Thread, Route 2, Box 118, Pineville, KY 40977.

West of Chenoa in Frakes is the Henderson Settlement, a United Methodist ministry started in 1925 as a school and community outreach center. Now Henderson Settlement is a multipurpose community service facility and the only Methodist mission in the country with an agricultural development program—1,300 acres of land, livestock, orchards, gardens, and a big community greenhouse. The old high school houses a library, offices, and a weaving room where people can learn and pursue the craft. Weavings and other locally made crafts are sold in The Log House Craft Shop (606–337–5823). Visitors are welcome to tour the settlement or to come for an extended stay for a retreat or work camp. Call ahead for reservations at (606) 337–3613.

The Red Bird Mission in Beverly is another similar United Methodist mission complex with a school, hospital, community outreach program, work camps, and a craft shop. Go back to Pineville and follow Highway 66 north for 26 miles. From the Daniel Boone Parkway, take Exit 34 and go south on Highway 66 into town. Directly across the street from the mission hospital is **Red Bird Mission Crafts,** in operation since 1921. The area craftspeople represented here are especially skilled at making hickory bark furniture, exquisite willow baskets, and handwoven rugs. Hours are 10:00 A.M. to 4:00 P.M., Monday through Saturday. You can reach the craft shop at (606) 598–2709.

Head northeast on Highway 119 to Harlan, a little mountain town populated primarily by people of Welsh descent. Natives say that since the Welsh have always been fantastic vocalists, it's no surprise that Harlan's fame is musical. The Harlan Boys' Choir, an all-male, award-winning choir, recently received national acclaim after performing at the inauguration of President George Bush. What most people don't know is that the choir is an offshoot of a 1945 girls' group called The Harlan Musettes, now under the direction of Marilyn Schraeder (606–573–3577). David Davies (606–573–3559) directs the boys, who range from third grade through high school. The repertoire is classical, and the sound is exquisite. Stop by the school to catch a rehearsal or call a director for the performance schedule.

Another Harlan original is the Poke Sallet Festival, held during the last week in June. The festival affords you plenty of opportunities to eat poke sallet, barbecued chicken, and corn pone and buttermilk, a mountain meal if there ever was one. Poke sallet is a cold salad of very young poke plant leaves (which are bitter and mildly poisonous when the plant is several months older); the leaves are cooked way down, like turnip greens, and have a flavor similar to asparagus. They're said to have healing powers. Call (606) 573–4717 for more festival information.

If you're staying overnight, consider the Three Deer Inn Bed and Breakfast in nearby Putney. The house is a spacious cedar lodge at the base of Black Mountain with all the creature comforts. From Harlan, go east on Highway 119 to the 22-mile marker, cross a concrete bridge, and take the first road on the right; continue to bear right and look for the sign. Reservations are necessary. Write P.O. Drawer 299, Grays Knob, KY 40829, or call (606) 573–6666.

Head north of Harlan on Highway 421, straight up the mountain. At the summit of Pine Mountain you'll see a sign for **The Little Shepherd Trail,** a 38-mile-graveled trail that runs along the ridge of the 2,800-foot mountain all the way to Whitesburg. Midway is Kingdom Come State Park, near Cumberland. It's recommended that you use a four-wheel-drive vehicle, walk, take horses, or ride mountain bikes on the trail.

On the other side of Pine Mountain, make a hard right onto Highway 221, go east "a far piece" (in this case, about 10 miles), and turn onto Highway 510, then immediately into the driveway of the **Pine Mountain Settlement School.** The history of the place begins with an early settler named William Creech who recognized the need for a school similar to a settlement school in Hindman founded by Katherine Pettit, who based her ideas on Jane Addams's work in urban settings. From 1913 until 1972 the Pine Mountain School was a remarkably wholesome and successful school, community center, and medical facility.

After the regular school closed in 1972, the folks at Pine Mountain decided to flow with the real needs of the community and became an environmental education center. Good timing—eastern Kentucky was and is suffering massive exploitation in a nation tending toward overconsumption, waste of resources, overpopulation, and a general lack of concern and understanding for the fragile, crucial cycles of the natural world. More than 2,000 students a year come for hands-on, outdoor learning. A long waiting list indicates a greater need than this one small institution can fill. Write for more information: Pine Mountain Settlement School, Pine Mountain, KY 40810. Visitors are welcome to tour the fascinating campus.

The next major town to the east along Highway 119 is Cumberland. Downtown on West Main Street, across from the public library, is the Poor Fork Arts and Craft Guild, a shop for more than seventy-five members who make various craft items—everything from quilts to wooden trains. A trend throughout this region is to make crafts from coal. A tole painter may put a bright barnyard scene on the face of a big chunk of coal, and a carver may make small sculptures of miners from the dark, black, familiar material. Hours are Monday through Saturday, 10:00 A.M. to 6:00 P.M.; (606–589–2497).

Directly up the mountain from Cumberland is the **Kingdom Come State Park** (606–589–2479). From Cumberland take Route 1926 north and follow signs to the park. Here is another access point to the Little Shepherd Trail. The trail and the park are named after John Fox, Jr.'s famous novel about Appalachian life, *The Little Shepherd of Kingdom Come*. In 1903 Fox's book was the first American novel to sell more than one million copies. This park is known for its incredible vistas and rich mountain woodlands. Two of the most spectacular sites are the Log Rock—a natural rock arch that looks like a log—and Raven Rock, a huge hunk of stone that thrusts some 290 feet into the air and has a capacious sand cave at its base that is used as an amphitheater for concerts and theatrical performances. Stop by the visitors' center for trail maps.

Still heading east along the gap line, Highway 119 leads to Letcher County. As you wind along the Cumberland River bottom, watch for Highway 932 on the right (east) side of the road. Turn and go 1⁷⁄₁₀ miles to the entrance of the **Bad Branch Nature Preserve** on the left. This place is so special that I barely have the nerve to include it here, but if you visit, you must promise to treat it with great care, to soak it into your soul, and to support nature preserves here and everywhere in any way that you are able. This gorge, rimmed by hundred-foot cliffs, is home to an especially unique ecosystem of rare plant species and breathtaking wildflowers. The trail leads you through a hemlock and rhododendron kingdom along some of the only clean, pure water you're going to see. At the end is a spectacular, 60-foot waterfall arching over the edge of a sandstone cliff.

Get back on Highway 119 and head north (turn right) over Pine Mountain into Whitesburg. Don't neglect to stop at one of the high lookout points where you can get a more abstract sense of the texture and shape of the land. You'll also get a very concrete sense of the meaning of "mountaintop removal," a method of strip-mining a seam(s) of coal by taking off whatever is above it, usually the entire top of a mountain. With this panorama before you, pay mental tribute to one of Letcher County's great native sons, the late Harry M. Caudill, writer, teacher, lawyer, politician, and outspoken activist in Appalachian social and economic issues. His historical writings, like *Night Comes to the Cumberlands* and *Theirs Be the Power*, are disturbing and powerful books about the troubled power relations in these mountains; in his storyteller (preserver) mode, Caudill has written a number of honest, intimate portraits of his people in books like *The Mountain, the Miner and the Lord.*

Downtown Whitesburg, next to the North Fork of the Kentucky River, is the **Appalshop** building, a community-oriented, not-for-profit arts and education center working to preserve traditional culture and history and to encourage conscientious involvement in contemporary arts and social issues. Open to visitors, Appalshop is best known for making powerful documentaries about folk culture figures and about social activism in Appalachia. While visiting, you can ask to watch almost any of their videos like "On Our Own Land," about the history and demise of the broad form deed in Kentucky, or "Chairmaker," about the life and work of Dewey Thompson, a furniture maker from Sugarloaf Hollow. The Headwaters Television series is a weekly broadcast of these documentaries on public television.

June Appal Recordings, Appalshop's own record label, has also made a massive cultural contribution by making recordings of Appalachian musicians and storytellers, famous and obscure, ranging from contemporary folk dulcimer artists like John McCutcheon and traditional mountain banjo players like Morgan Sexton (who won a National Heritage Award from the National Endowment for the Arts in 1990) to mountain storytellers like Ray Hicks. Appalshop's Roadside Theatre is a small theater/storytelling troupe that delights and instructs folks all over the region. Appalshop also runs a community radio station, WMMT 88.7 FM, to which you are hereby commanded to tune-in while in the area. Like the river, Appalshop's efforts flow out into the whole Kentucky-Virginia area, giving us all an education and renewed sense of pride and hope. For literature and catalogs, write: Appalshop, 306 Madison Street, Whitesburg, KY 41858, or call (606) 633–0108.

While you're in Whitesburg have a meal downtown at the Courthouse Café (606–633–5859), a charming little restaurant that serves healthy, delicious lunches and dinners made from scratch; try the baked turkey breast sandwiches, large salads, or ever-changing special meals. Josephine Richardson, one of the owners, acts as dealer for a number of local artists and craftspeople. The quilts, wood carvings, paintings, and photographs displayed in the restaurant are for sale. Hours are 10:00 A.M. to 8:30 P.M., Monday through Friday. While you dine, read through a copy of the local paper, *The Mountain Eagle.* There's a very democratic section, usually on page B4, called "Speak Your Piece" for which you anonymously call an answering machine, and the editor prints, verbatim, what you say. The "pieces" range from heated discussions about the war in Saudi Arabia or layoffs at the coal mines to "I hate my boyfriend's guts and I hope he knows it."

One of the woodcarvers represented at the Café and on many a desk at Appalshop is James Bloomer. Take Highway 931 south through Whitco and turn right (west) on Highway 588. You'll see his little red shop in front of his white frame house in a very deep curve in the road. Most of his work is in buckeye, a wood that is almost white at the carving stage, but gets lovely gray streaks as it ages and dries. He carves all sorts of animals, but highly detailed decoys are his forte. You can call him at (606) 633–4279.

On the west side of the county in a community called Blackey is an area museum disguised as a general store, the **C. B. Caudill Store** (606–633–7738). From Whitesburg, take Highway 15 north, then turn on Highway 7 south toward Isom. The store is just past Blackey on the right. Usually a few fellows are chatting on the big front porch. The store, which opened in 1933, is now owned by Joe Begley, an upbeat, dedicated activist who has used his store to unite diverse groups over such issues as the 77th Strip Mining Bill and the area health clinic. "Everyone should be a politician," he says. "Even Christ was a protestor, and a strong one at that." The walls of the store tell some of their own stories. Joe has intentionally collected mining artifacts—everything from hats, boots, lights, and tools to "scrip," old mine company currency useful only within the mining camps. His *unintentional* collections are amusing—scan the shelves for things like fifty-year-old tubes of hair-restoration creme.

Ask Joe Begley or the folks at Appalshop about the Carcassonne dance. Once or twice a month at the Carcassonne community center people get together for a big square dance, the traditional kind with a caller and usually a live "house" band. Mountain squares and contra lines are so unique that even if you're an experienced country dancer, this will be a challenge. Just listen and have fun. From the C. B. Caudill Store, stay on Highway 7 for a few hundred yards and turn right on the first road on the right, Elk Creek Road. Follow the pavement to the very top of the mountain.

Back on Highway 7, go west past Blackey and the store, turn south on Highway 1103 and follow the signs to the **Lilley Cornett Woods.** Because this is one of the few old-growth forests in the state, it is of great value to ecological researchers and to beauty-addicts alike. The wise and eccentric Lilley Cornett purchased this land after World War I and did not allow any live timber to be cut except for blighted chestnuts. His children continued the tradition, and finally in 1969 the state purchased the land and continues to preserve it. Time is the key. Old-growth forests are characterized by a large number of trees more than 200 years old, many of which are of great commercial value.

In order to protect the forest, visitors are not allowed to hike without a guide. The guides, however, are real treats, and they will take you out whenever you arrive. You'll learn more in an hour hiking with these folks than you could in a year reading dendrology books. Come between 9:00 A.M. and 5:00 P.M. From May 15 to August 15 the woods are open daily, and in April, May, September, and October, they are open only on weekends. Contact: Superintendent, Lilley Cornett Woods, HC 63, Box 2710, Skyline, KY 41851, or call (606) 633–5828.

On the east end of Letcher County, very near the Virginia border on Highway 119 North, is a town called Jenkins, originally a mining camp built by Consolidation Coal Company—note the rows of identical houses. On the east side of town, watch on the left for Whitaker Music Store, an old, run-down music store with a surprising collection of old albums, sheet music, books, and a few instruments. The rock 'n' roll albums are funny, but there are some valuable items in Ervin Whitaker's country music collection. He's open from 9:00 A.M. to 5:00 P.M., Monday through Saturday.

Leave Jenkins and go east on Highway 119 into Pike County, the largest county in the state. South of Pikeville, in the center of the county on Highway 1789, is Fishtrap Lake, a large lake known for its largemouth bass, bluegill, and crappie. Directly south of Fishtrap Lake on the state border is the **Breaks Interstate Park,** where the Russell Fork River, a tributary of the Big Sandy, has done its darndest to imitate the Grand Canyon. For more than 5 miles the river canyon has high jagged walls, some exceeding 1,600 feet in height. Unlike the Grand Canyon, this gorge is lush and tree covered. It is believed to have been formed primarily during the late Paleozoic era, some 250 million years ago. The park has four fantastic overlooks, one of which is at the Rhododendron Lodge and Restaurant. Contact: Breaks Interstate Park, P.O. Box 100, Breaks, VA 24607, or call (703) 865–4413.

Pike County is known nationally as the locale of the infamous Hatfield-McCoy feud, a violent interfamily vendetta that began during the Civil War and was sustained until almost the turn of the century. Buried in Pikeville in the Dils Cemetery are several major figures in the feud on the McCoy side. This cemetery was the first in eastern Kentucky to be integrated. Take the Bypass Road to the east side of town; the cemetery is north of the Bypass's split with Highway 1460 on the east side of the road. For more information, contact Ms. William Forsyth at (606) 437–7203.

Much is made of the Pikeville Cut-Thru, a massive rerouting of highways, railroads, and rivers on the west side of town. After fourteen years of labor, millions of dollars, and millions of tons of blasted and hauled rock and dirt, the cut-through was completed in 1987. You have to see it to believe it. For the best view, take the Bypass Road to the northwest side of town, turn uphill on Oak Lane, and curve around to Cedar Drive. For more information on this huge project, stop by the visitors' center at 101 Huffman Avenue between 8:30 A.M. and 4:00 P.M., or call (606) 432–5504.

Big Sandy Country

Johnson County's history involves some outstanding women. Country music stars Crystal Gayle and Loretta Lynn are both Johnson County natives. Loretta Lynn was born and raised in a beautiful setting in **Butcher Hollow,** near Van Lear. From Paintsville take Highway 23 south to Highway 302, turn east and follow the signs to the board and batten cabin where Lynn lived. The place was rebuilt for the filming of the movie *Coal Miner's Daughter,* a biography of the singer's difficult but triumphant life. Remnants of an orchard make the place feel authentic. The site is open to visitors all year.

In Van Lear's tiny downtown in the former Consolidated Coal Company office building is the Van Lear Historical Society Museum. If you haven't yet seen a real-life mining camp, check out the model of a typical company town in the museum. Hours are 9:00 A.M. to 3:00 P.M., Monday through Saturday, from March through November.

Another legendary woman is Jenny Wiley, an early settler of the Big Sandy area who survived a remarkably tragic capture by Shawnee Indians and subsequent escape. She died at age seventy-one and is buried in a cemetery 5 miles south of Paintsville on Highway 23 near the site of Harmon Station, the first white settlement in eastern Kentucky. Mathias Harmon was one of the hunter/Indian fighters now known as "Long Hunters" because of the length of their sojourns in the wilderness. In 1750 he and his companions built a fortlike log hunting lodge on this site; in the late 1780s, they built a more permanent block house.

The trail that Wiley and the Indians followed was once well worn and cleared, but had disappeared into the undergrowth until recently. The 180-mile Jenny Wiley Trail has been restored and is now marked for hikers. You can access the trail from Greenbow Lake, Carter Caves, and Jenny Wiley state parks. If you want to hike the whole trail, you can start in South Portsmouth (Greenup County) and travel south. The best way to see eastern Kentucky is on foot on this trail, which roughly traces the Pottsville escarpment and runs through the gamut of sites; you see lush gorges, open farmland, strip mines, mountain towns, and miles and miles of woods. For more information on the Jenny Wiley Trail, contact the **Jenny Wiley State Resort Park** (800–325–0142 or 606–886–2711) between Paintsville and Prestonsburg on Highway 3, east of Highway 23/460 on Dewey Lake, a clear lake famous for its white bass run (April only).

Each summer the Jenny Wiley Summer Music Theatre presents a colorful musical version of the legendary Jenny Wiley story and three Broadway musicals, such as "Hello Dolly" or "The Mystery of Edwin Drood." You can take in a different performance every night for four nights in a row. The outdoor performances are at the Jenny Wiley State Park in an amphitheater open from late June through mid-August, Tuesday through Sunday, with curtain time at 8:00 P.M. Call (606) 886–9274 for further information.

The David community, about 6 miles southwest of Prestonsburg on Highway 404, has two surprises in store for you. One is a small crafts shop called David Appalachian Crafts; it features quality traditional mountain crafts like split oak baskets, wood carvings, and quilts. Hours are 9:00 A.M. to 4:00 P.M., Monday through Friday. Write them at: Highway 404, David, KY 41616, or call (606) 886–2377. Also in town is the David School, a nonsectarian, not-for-profit, wonderful school committed to educating local high school dropouts from low-income families. In 1972, Dan Greene founded the school in an old mining camp with hopes of helping kids who were functionally illiterate. Now more than 95 percent of the David School students have finished their high school education, and there's always a waiting list. Other schools around the state and nation are finally looking to Greene's program as a model. If you are inspired, stop by.

Due south of the David School is a longer-lived educational institution built upon similar hopes. Alice Lloyd College was founded in 1917 by Alice Lloyd, a Radcliffe graduate who contracted spinal meningitis at the age of forty and moved with her mother to the mountains of Kentucky, expecting to die. Despite her illness Alice Lloyd typed letters with her left hand to business people and friends in Boston, asking for help in establishing a school. Lloyd lived until 1962, and her school flourished on the hillsides of Caney Creek Valley where it stands today. To reach the school, take Highway 7 south, then Highway 899 southwest into Pippa Passes in Knott County.

Alice Lloyd gave her students a free education with one string attached—she requested that after the students receive their full professional training, they return to eastern Kentucky to work and live. Almost 4,000 graduates have become teachers in the region and more than 1,000 have become mountain doctors and other professionals. Visitors are welcome to the beautiful campus all year.

A few miles away on Highway 550, slightly south of Highway 80, is Hindman and, strung along Troublesome Creek, the Hindman Settlement School, yet another educational facility that has been a social and cultural goldmine. The school was founded in 1902 on the folk school plan and operated successfully for many years. Like other settlement schools, it is now closed and has had to serve the community in new ways. Today it hosts some of the best workshops in the state on traditional dance and mountain crafts and culture. Visitors can tour the campus free, Monday through Friday between 8:00 A.M. and 5:00 P.M. You'll see a film about Jean Ritchie, the nationally acclaimed folk musician and composer from the nearby town of Viper.

After all this talk of mountain crafts, it's incarnation time. To meet a master of the "fine craft" of white oak basket-making, take Highway 160 for about 3 miles north out of Hindman toward Vest. Byrd Owsley has been making strong, shapely, split white oak baskets since he can remember. Byrd will explain the process and is glad to sell a few from his home. Watch the right side (east) of the road for a small cluster of houses on the mountain side of the creek; there's a small car bridge in the middle, and Byrd's mailbox has his name on it.

Proceed about 2 miles past the junction of Highways 1087 and

160. Just 20 yards past the sign that says AT THE END YOU MEET GOD, turn right (east) up a steep blacktopped driveway to the **Quicksand Craft Center** (606–785–5230). These folks are widely renowned for their fine weaving. When Shakertown at Pleasant Hill (Mercer County) was being restored, these weavers were commissioned to make complex reproduction rugs, runners, and coverlets for the museum. If you're in the market for a high-quality handmade rug, pay a visit Monday through Friday between 8:00 A.M. and 5:00 P.M.

You're in store for more regional crafts and an architectural museum of sorts at the Pioneer Village, south of Hindman. Take Highway 160 south to Carr Fork Lake, then take Highway 15 south just over 2 miles into Red Fox and watch the east side of the road for the long driveway to the village. This group of cabins was moved to this location in Rainbow Hollow when the Carr Fork Dam was built. Some of the log structures date as far back as the 1780s. Presently the cabins are standing, but the logs are not chinked (filled in with mud, rock, straw, etc.). The craft shop, which pays for the cabins' maintenance, features local handmade crafts sold on consignment. Ask to see the cornhusk dolls made by folk singer Jean Ritchie's sisters, Kitty, Mallie, and Jewel. Hours are Monday through Saturday, 10:00 A.M. to 6:00 P.M. Call (606) 642–3650.

Nearby Hazard is a booming little riverside town at the end of the Daniel Boone Parkway. Because it sits on and near some of the widest, richest seams of coal in the area, coal is at the heart of almost everything here, a fact made loud and clear during the third weekend of September when Hazard hosts the Black Gold Festival. In town, spend a little time at the Hazard Perry County Museum at 234 Walnut Street, next door to the visitors' information center (606–439–2659). This free museum is a visual history book of the area from the nineteenth century through World War II. Hours are 10:00 A.M. to 4:00 P.M. every day but Wednesday and Saturday, when it opens at 1:00 P.M., and Sunday when it's closed. Call (606) 439–4325.

Let me be devious and point out a more modern artifact of history. Go north of town on Highway 15 and turn onto Dawahare Drive and into the Holiday Inn parking lot. The ground under the west wing of the building is sinking, so the building is collapsing as if it had been in an earthquake. It wasn't. The east part of the inn is built on natural, solid rock while the west disaster was built on "fill," rock and dirt added to fill the area—a process some engineers believe can be done on reclaimed mine sites.

To get an inside look at mining, make reservations with the Hazard Vocational School to tour their underground mock mine. The displays begin by portraying early crude mining methods and progress through time to show the present-day method of long wall mining. Call the Tourist Commission at (606) 439–2659 for more information. To get to the Vocational School, take North Main Street north until it splits with Walker Avenue; take the latter to the end.

An architectural treat is in store 20 miles north of Hazard in Buckhorn on Highway 28, which is off Highway 15 North. The Log Cathedral, now functioning as the Buckhorn Lake Area Church, is an unusually large and beautiful log structure built in 1907 as part of the Witherspoon College campus. Harvey S. Murdoch of the Society of Soul Winners helped found a Christian elementary and high school and called it a college in order to give the students extra status. The massive logs are white oak, cut from the surrounding woods. Inside, the space is lovely and impressive. The gem in the crown of the cathedral is a Hook and Hasting pipe organ that has recently been restored and sounds great. Visitors are welcome between 9:00 A.M. and 5:00 P.M. daily. Call (606) 398–7245.

From Hazard, take Highway 421 south about 20 miles to Hyden. Like the mountain schools in the area, **Frontier Nursing Services** near Hyden is an institution committed to promoting health and growth. Mary Breckinridge started Frontier Nursing as a school in 1925. Her original students and the generations of nurses that followed have made strong impressions on the minds of everyone who has encountered them riding on horseback to remote hollers and mountain towns to deliver babies and adminster health care. Folks at Frontier Nursing have revised their charter and are also involved in child care, general education, and regional economics. The grounds are lovely, and the history of the service is inspirational. Make sure to go in the chapel, which has a fifteenth-century Flemish stained-glass window, and to see the Wendover Big House, a log home built in 1925 for the founder. Call ahead to take a tour or to make reservations for meals and accommodations (606–672–2317). Frontier Nursing is in Wendover, south of Hyden off Highway 80.

If I were giving an award for the best town name in the state, the prize would have to go to Leslie County's Hell Fer Certain, a little not-even-on-the-map community north of Hyden off Highway 257. Runners-up in the area would include Devil's Jump Branch, Confluence, Cutshin, Thousandsticks, Yeaddis, Smilax, Yerkes, and Krypton.

The Gorgeous Gorge

The Red River Gorge, in the northern end of the Daniel Boone National Forest 60 miles east of Lexington on the Bert T. Combs Mountain Parkway, is one of the most beautiful and best-loved wilderness areas in Kentucky. Actually the area was quite obscure until its existence was threatened in the late 1960s by a proposed 5,000-acre impoundment on the Red River's North Fork. Intense controversy raged until 1975 when the plan was nixed. All the publicity caused the park to be badly overused by visitors who weren't ecologically sensitive. Today the park has been reorganized; large areas are strictly protected, and visitor education is an important part of forest management.

The Gorge was formed by erosion and weathering, in much the same way that the Grand Canyon was carved out by the Colorado River. The North Fork of Red River cut through the area more than 340 million years ago and left behind some fantastic geologic formations in limestone, conglomerate sandstone, and siltstone, all of which are tucked under a layer of shale. The most outstanding phenomena are eighty natural rock arches, a number surpassed in the United States only by Arches National Park in Utah.

A good place to begin exploring the Gorge is **Natural Bridge State Resort Park** (606–663–2214), a full-fledged state park with a big lodge, cottages, camping, a pool, recreation areas, and a spectacular natural stone bridge. This park is not very isolated, but it can serve as a point of reference for outings to more remote places. From Interstate 64, take the Bert T. Combs Mountain Parkway southeast about 50 miles, get off at the Slade Interchange onto Highway 11, and follow signs to the park.

On the way in or out, you should have a meal at **Miguel's Pizza,** a little building with a carved wooden front door, on the left near the park entrance. Miguel's parents, who live next door, grow an enormous and wonderful garden. Order a veggie pizza and you'll be likely to find it laced with whatever's in season—heav-

Natural Stone Bridge

enly. If you're a climber, this is the only store in the area that sell a good variety of climbing supplies. Miguel's is open most weekends (except during the winter) and whenever people are out and about.

On the west side of Miguel's you may notice a rambling shamble of buildings by the side of the road, one of which is a snake pit with a fancy name, the Miami Valley Serpentarium (606–663–9160). You've always secretly wanted to see one of these places—here's your chance to indulge. It's safe. Besides, if you aren't from this area, you may never have seen some of the snakes and reptiles we have here. If you're lucky, you'll visit on a day when they're doing "live demonstrations." I'll leave the rest to your imagination. Hours are Monday through Saturday, noon to 8:00 P.M., and Sunday, noon to 6:00 P.M., from June through

August. From October through December and March and April, it's open on weekends from 11:00 A.M. to 5:00 P.M. It is closed in September, January, February, and May, except for chance openings on weekends when the weather is good.

A designated driving loop winds through the area beginning in Nada, a mile and a half west of the Slade Interchange of the Parkway on Highway 15. Take Highway 77 north through the Nada Tunnel, a 10-foot-wide, 13-foot-tall, 800-foot-long tunnel cut by hand in 1877 to give small gauge trains access to the big timber in the area. Stay on Highway 77 and it will run into Highway 715, which runs parallel to the river. At Pine Ridge, Highway 715 connects with Highway 15 again, which leads back to Natural Bridge. Ask for a map in the lodge at Natural Bridge.

Big timber is the subject of a small museum in the recently restored Gladie Creek Cabin, which you'll pass on the loop drive. This was the 1884 cabin of John Ledford, who bought and logged more than 4,000 acres here. The Forest Service recently rebuilt the cabin and filled it with historic objects that refer to the early years of the logging industry in eastern Kentucky, including log branding irons, tools, models of old equipment, and historic photographs.

Gladie Creek Historical Site also serves as a Visitors' Information Center (606–745–3100) for the north end of the Daniel Boone Forest. This is another good place to get trail maps, weather reports, and general advice about hiking or anything else concerning the National Forest. Hours are 10:00 A.M. to 6:00 P.M. from Memorial Day to Labor Day or by appointment. If you're not on the driving loop, you can reach Gladie Creek from the north. Take Highway 77 south to Highway 715; go east for about 11 miles and watch for the cabin on the right side of the road.

The absolute best way to be in the Gorge is to be hiking, for driving does not do the woods justice. You must sweat, propel yourself by your own energy, drink when you're thirsty, eat when you're hungry (or can't wait any longer for the granola bar), feel the leaves brush against your legs, feel the sunshine on your shoulders when you come to an opening in the forest canopy, hear and see the animals, and so taste the life of the mountains. More than 165 miles of foot trails in the Daniel Boone Forest give you ample opportunity to be here the right way. Get maps from the Hemlock Lodge at Natural Bridge or at Gladie or anywhere you see a ranger. Hike as many trails as you're able.

The Sheltowee Trace (Trail #100) is the only backpacking trail that traverses the entire length of the Daniel Boone National Forest. It stretches 257 miles through nine counties, beginning in Rowan County in the north and ending in Tennessee, where it connects with the John Muir Trail (named for the father of the Sierra Club), which, in turn, connects to the great Appalachian Trail. If you're planning a backpacking trip, check with a ranger. The trail is marked with a white diamond or turtle-shaped blaze. The world "Sheltowee" is Shawnee for Big Turtle, Daniel Boone's Indian name when he was captured and adopted by the Shawnee Chief Blackfish.

The Pioneer Weapons Hunting Area is a 7,480-acre area in the National Forest, north of the Gorge, designated for hunting deer, turkey, grouse, and squirrel, BUT, you must use only primitive weapons—black powder muzzle loaders, bows and arrows, blow guns, spears, rubberbands, whatever. Before you hunt, be sure to call the forest supervisor (606–745–3100) so that you understand the regulations.

From Frenchburg, which is in the heart of the National Forest near the Pioneer Weapon Hunting Area, take Highway 36 north, then Highway 1274 east for 2⁹⁄₁₀ miles to the first paved road on the right (south), marked only by a small brown sign that says SPRATT STONEWORKS. Turn and bear left onto a gravel road, then left again until you find yourself at a third fork in the road. Go to the brick house on the hill and ask for Verne Spratt, the old man who owns the land where there are a number of curious and well-preserved stoneworks and earthen constructions. The Kentucky Heritage Council gave Spratt a grant to preserve the site and to develop a trail.

The large stone effigy or geometrical construction is thought to be a serpent mound, but this has not been proven archaeologically. It's a strange series of stone walls completely blanketed in moss. To the southeast is a group of more than twenty small stone mounds, some linear, some round or ovate. Because the land surrounding these constructions is not arable, it's unlikely that these were built by white farmers. They are probably prehistoric; a number of stone mounds found in this region have been dated to the Middle and Late Woodland periods. Mr. Spratt is likely to tell you stories about how John Swift's hidden silver mines are nearby. He can point out eighteenth-century graffiti on the rocks and will read to you from Swift's diary, which names rock formations that seem to correspond with some of those on his farm. Although it isn't necessary, it is best to call ahead (606–768–0202). This is guaranteed to be a strange adventure, something that will pique your curiosity forever.

In downtown Frenchburg at the intersection of Highways 460 and 36 is the Corner Restaurant (606–768–2844), a big social spot and the place to get down-home cooking. Stop in for coffee if nothing else because the dining area is decorated with parts of old stills, farm machinery, hand-painted porcelain cafeteria-style plates, and more. If you've got the traveling blues, these friendly folks will lift your spirits. Another place for good eating is a few blocks west on Highway 460 (Main Street), in a little white clapboard house that has been converted into Mom's Country Kitch'n (606–768–6232).

If you turn toward the north from the Corner Restaurant on Highway 36, take the first street to the right, and follow it to the end—you'll see a trail going up the hillside. This leads to Donathan Rock, a great huge rock teetering near the edge of a cliff, from which you get a perfect aerial view of Frenchburg below. Park in town and walk over. A mile farther north on Highway 36 brings you to the Roe Wells School. Watch carefully for it on the left—the sign is small. The school is a typical one-room country schoolhouse and quaint as can be. Look in the windows; the old desks and books, chalkboard, and even a few messages from the teacher remain. It would make a perfect movie set. If you want to go inside, make an appointment by calling (606) 768–3323.

Leaving Frenchburg in the southeasterly direction, you will find two surprises in store. Take Highway 460 east for 3 miles and look on the right side of the road for Barton's Foods, Manufacturer of Relish, Sorghum, and Jellies. Charlotte Roe is glad to show visitors around the operation. Your nose will tell you what's cooking at the moment. One day it's a hot chowchow relish; next, it's cinnamon and pear preserves (which tastes like apple pie); and the next it's old mill molasses, Delano Roe's opus magnum. Barton's is best known for Moonshine Jelly, which contains 10 percent Georgia Moon. Many of Barton's delectables are available for sale. Hours are 8:00 A.M. to 4:30 P.M., Monday through Friday. Call (606) 768–3750.

One mile east of Barton's is the **Swamp Valley Store and Museum.** The humor around here runs thick, but it's all deeply rooted in the history of the area. Clayton Wells, the jovial owner, was a pack rat from his youth, and now it's paid off. He kept every little thing of his and his family's and other folks', too. In the last twenty years or so, Clayton has restored and moved a whole slew of historic buildings onto the property near his country store. He filled each one with appropriate artifacts, and voila! a museum. What makes the place outstanding (and funny) is his accompanying stories. "My people always told about . . ."

The main museum house, for example, was the home of John Poplin, Clayton's great-great-grandfather, a slave driver who brought slaves from Sand Gap, Virginia, to Lexington, Kentucky. Other buildings include an old metal silo called "Photo Silo," which could be a twist on the little drive-in photo-developing units that sit in mall parking lots, but it's not. Inside are school photos of every child in Menifee County for fifty years. Clayton and his friends also record music here and sell square dance tapes for $10. They're pretty good. Other buildings include the E-Z Rest Casket Shop, full of authentic tools for blacksmithing, shoe repair, stone masonry, and casket-making, and the Cheese Shop, supplied with everything necessary to make cheese, except milk. There's more, but you have to visit Swamp Valley to appreciate it. It's worth the drive. Even Garrison Keillor stopped by once to do a little historical research. Keillor wanted to verify the record-breaking length of the marriage of Lynn Boyd Wells and Alydia Rupe Wells, Clayton's oldest uncle and aunt. They were married something like eighty-two years! Amen.

You are still in beautiful country when you travel to the south side of the Red River Gorge. From Natural Bridge, head south on Highway 11 through Zachariah and Zoe (my name town and the site of my worst bicycle wreck) to Beattyville. This friendly little mountain town has the best-named restaurant in the world, The Purple Cow, on Main Street. Eat any meal there any day of the week, just for the fun of it. The last weekend in October, Beattyville is host to the world's only festival devoted to the humblest of all creatures, the wooly worm. Call (606) 464–8517 for festival information. The town's most important claim to fame, however, is that it is the place where all three forks, North, Middle, and South, converge to form the Kentucky River.

Grass Roots Crafts, south of Jackson in Breathitt County on Highway 15, is the place to see craftspeople in action. As the name implies, this is a cooperative effort. They're housed in a log cabin where people pursue all kinds of crafts from woodworking to weaving. The specialty here is quilting and appliqué work, and finished quilts are for sale at the shop, Monday through Saturday, 8:00 A.M. to 6:00 P.M. (606–666–7371).

From Highway 15 south, veer off to the southeast on Highway 476 to the **Robinson Forest,** a large research and educational forest owned and managed by the University of Kentucky. Visitors can take a self-guided hike along a nature trail to see a wide variety of flora and fauna that are typical of this area. A climb up the Camp Robinson Lookout Tower is worth the effort. To get to the tower, take Highway 426 into the forest about 5 miles past the Buckhorn Church at the edge of the university's property, and turn left on Clemons Road to the tower trail. Call (606) 666–5034 for more information.

From Jackson, head west on Highway 30 into a little community called Lerose, home of the **Pioneer Museum,** where there is a restored 1874 homestead. All the buildings are log and are filled with period furnishings and tools. You can tour a smokehouse, complete with meat and vegetable preserving containers, a shophouse, an Indian artifact exhibit, and a residence, the 1806 William Moore House, the first home built within the city limits of nearby Booneville. The museum is open from April 1 to October 30, Friday and Saturday from 9:00 A.M. to 5:00 P.M., Sunday from 1:00 to 5:00 P.M., or by appointment; call (606) 593–5937.

Annville Crafts and the Brockman Weavers' loomhouse is in Jackson County on Highway 30, southeast of the Daniel Boone National Forest's S Tree area in Annville. These folks are known for producing very fine woven items and for giving informative demonstrations. When you touch their work, I guarantee that you'll want to learn to weave. A few finished items are always kept on hand for retail sales, and visitors are welcome to come by from 9:00 A.M. to 4:00 P.M., Monday through Saturday, year-round. Call (606) 364–5084.

Iron Country

If these United States can be called a body,
Kentucky can be called its heart.

These words are from the first stanza of "Kentucky Is My Land," a poem by the late poet laureate of Kentucky, Jesse Stuart, a wholesome, hopeful writer whose work is deeply rooted in his given place. Because W-Hollow was Stuart's home and place of inspiration, the area has been made into a kind of pastoral museum and maintained as Stuart knew it—cattle graze in some pastures, and young forests are being allowed to grow to maturity. The **Jesse Stuart State Nature Preserve** lies between Highways 1 and 2 west of Greenup off Highway 23. Visitors can walk the hills and fields Stuart walked and visit Op's Cabin, the old white clapboard house where he did most of his writing. For those who know his work, the fictional Laurel Ridge is Seaton Ridge. His home is also on the preserve but is private property. The Kentucky State Nature Preserves Commission (502–564–2886) jointly maintains the place with the Jesse Stuart Foundation, a nonprofit organization devoted to preserving and sharing Stuart's work. The grocery store in Greenup has most of Stuart's books on display and for sale near the checkout line. To order books, contact the foundation at P.O. Box 391, Ashland, KY 41114, or call (606) 329–5232.

Continue south on Highway 1 to the Greenbo Lake State Resort Park (606–473–7324), where the lodge is named after Jesse Stuart. On the last weekend in September the park hosts a Jesse Stuart Weekend during which speakers lecture on the life and works of Stuart, a guided tour of W-Hollow is given, films are shown, and exhibits are open. In addition, Greenbo Lake is said to be marvelous for fishing, its dining room is popular, and camping is available.

Nine miles south of the park at the intersection of Highways 1 and 3111 is the Oldtown covered bridge, spanning the Little Sandy River near the site of a former Shawnee village. The 194-foot long, two-span Burr-type bridge was built in 1880 and has not been restored. **Bennett's Mill Bridge** has one less span and is one foot longer and twenty-five years older than the Oldtown bridge, AND it's functional. It was built in 1855 for access to Bennett's Grist Mill on Tygart Creek. What is amazing is that the original frame and footings are intact. This bridge is on Highway 7, west of the Greenup County Locks and Dam. (Warning: Grays Branch Road, the direct route from the dam, is a rough, dirt logging road.)

From the bridge or from the nature preserve or park, go east to the edge of the Ohio River and take Highway 23 south. Before you reach the county border, you'll see a town called Russell between the road and the Ohio River. The town grew around the Russell Yard, the second-largest rail yard in the world—the largest is in

Japan—and the largest that is privately owned (by CSX Transportation, Inc.). The Russell YMCA, open since 1897, was originally built as a boardinghouse for men who worked railroad cars up and down the line. In 1989 Albert Riggs bought the YMCA and changed the name to **Albert's** (606–836–4344). When you enter town, just past the train overpass watch for an alley with a sign that says HISTORIC ALBERT'S INN and points you toward a three-story brick building in a big open lot by the tracks. Although the inn and cafeteria are primarily used by rail workers, they're open to the public. You won't find cheaper lodging or a more flexible meal schedule, and the place is living history. (Some retired railmen live here full time.) Rooms cost $13–$15 per night and $30–$50 per week. These days women are also welcome. The cafeteria is famous for its breakfasts, but it serves all meals. Hours are from 6:00 A.M. to 8:00 P.M. seven days a week; on Friday and Saturday breakfast is served until midnight. Bring your church bulletin in on Sunday, and get 10 percent off meals.

Ashland, the largest city in Kentucky east of Lexington, is at the junction of Highways 23 and 60, north of Interstate 64 on the West Virginia border. Ashland is headquarters for Ashland Oil and Armco Steel (not to mention that it's the hometown of country music stars Naomi and Wynonna Judd). Downtown you'll notice a surprising number of large ornate houses built by early industrialists during the last half of the nineteenth century. My favorite is at 1600 Central Avenue. The highest peaks of the roof sport two cast-iron dragons, like French *faîtages* or the figures on ancient Macedonian tombs, meant to ward off evil spirits. It was originally built at the corner of Winchester Avenue and Seventeenth Street but was hauled intact to the present site some twenty years later by a team of mules! The dragons did their job.

Another awesome building is the Mayo Manor, circa 1917, at the corner of Bath and Sixteenth streets. It now houses the **Kentucky Highlands Museum,** but even without the museum items, the mansion would be worth touring. Make sure to climb the grand staircase to the third floor where there is a large panel of handsome stained glass in the ceiling. The museum is organized by subject and period and ranges from exhibits of Adena, Fort Ancient, and Hopewell Indian cultures to rail, steam, and industrial histories, the evolution of radio, a World War II room, an impressive antique clothing collection, and a changing special exhibition on the third floor that usually is worth a visit in itself. Hours are 10:00

A.M. to 4:00 P.M., Tuesday through Saturday, and 1:00 to 4:00 P.M. on Sunday, except holidays. Admission is charged. Call (606) 329–8888.

Ashland's oldest and most traditional restaurant, Chimney Corner Tea Room (606–324–3300), is up the street from the museum on Carter Avenue between Sixteenth and Seventeenth streets. Fare includes rainbow trout, prime rib, really tasty sandwiches, and homemade desserts. Hours are 10:30 A.M. to 9:00 P.M. Monday through Friday, 9:00 A.M. to 9:00 P.M. on Saturday, and 9:00 A.M. to 8:00 P.M. on Sunday. One block away is Central Park, a forty-seven-acre area set aside when Ashland was laid-out in the 1850s; it contains a number of ancient Indian mounds that have been restored to their original proportions. They were found to contain human bones, pottery, and other artifacts that correspond with the Adena period (800 B.C. to A.D. 800).

For more contemporary local human artifacts, try the Ashland Area Art Gallery (606–329–1826) in the old Crump and Field Building, circa 1892, at the corner of Greenup Avenue and Fourteenth Street. The whole store front is cast iron! The gallery changes exhibits monthly and features regional artists. Hours are 10:00 A.M. to 4:00 P.M., Tuesday through Saturday, and 1:00 to 4:00 P.M. on Sunday.

Architecture buffs, brace yourselves. **The Piedmont Arts Center** (606–324–3175) at 1300 Winchester Avenue is out of this world. Art deco has never been better, and the people of Ashland cared enough to give this place an enormous face-lift (but what a face!). If you're in town on a night when a cultural event is scheduled, go, no matter what's playing. They book everything from Marcel Marceau to the Sistine Chapel Choir to Ray Charles. Or you can just tour the building between 10:00 A.M. and 4:30 P.M., Monday through Friday. In the early 1920s Paramount–Famous Lasky Corporation planned to build a chain of "talking picture" theaters like the Piedmont across the nation to showcase Piedmont Studios films. After a few theaters were built, the Depression hit and truncated their plan. In 1931 this joint was built for $400,000. The ceiling is painted with the famous art deco pseudo-Moravian sunburst surrounded by leaping gazelles. On the red walls are murals of sixteenth-century theatrical figures. The seats are done in plush red velvet. Ornamental pewter and brass are everywhere, even in the bathrooms. Next door is a small gallery/gift shop that is also open on Sunday from 1:00 to 5:00 P.M. Opulent is the word.

More opulence is in store for you at Irish Acres Antiques, a seemingly endless gallery filled with very fine American, European, and Asian antiques of all periods. The furniture will leave you wide-eyed, but don't fail to notice the significant details—glassware, silver, oriental rugs, and ceramics. To get there, leave Ashland via Interstate 64 west, get off at Exit 181 onto Highway 854 (also known as Jacks Fork Road), go into the town of Rush, and follow signs to Irish Acres. Call (606) 928–8502. This is a sister store to the Irish Acres Antiques in Nonesuch, owned by the same family and run with the same pizzazz. (See page 16.)

Two pig iron furnace ruins near Ashland are accessible to the public. One is the Clinton Furnace, built by the Poage brothers in 1833. From Ashland, take Highway 60 south, turn left (east) on Highway 538 and left again on Shopes Creek Road to the furnace ruins. The other, Princess Furnace, was put into operation in 1864. From Ashland, take Highway 60 east to Princess, turn north on Highway 5, and look immediately for a rough stone structure near the road.

Both furnaces were part of a much larger community of pig iron operations. Because the sites are usually in bad condition and none of them are part of guided tours, let me explain how they worked. It was a clumsy process, but these furnaces produced tons and tons of rough pig iron that was refined into steel, wrought iron, and ingot iron. The Civil War was fought with bullets and cannonballs from these humble industries. The earliest furnaces of the late eighteenth century produced approximately three tons of iron from nine tons of ore—today's steel furnaces need about one half hour to produce the same amount of steel the old furnaces could produce in a year.

Enormous stones were quarried from the nearby mountains and used to build the furnaces by the sides of hills. A bridge was built to the top of the chimney, into which they dumped the "charge," which consisted of iron ore, also mined locally, limestone, which acts as a fluxing agent, and charcoal, for hot heat. The charcoal was made by burning prime hardwood down to lumps of black, porous carbon. When all this was dumped into the top of the furnace, pig iron and slag came out the bottom and cooled in ditches. When you visit these old furnaces, climb inside, if possible, and look up the stack; often they taper beautifully to a small round opening at the top. In my opinion, the art of stonemasonry of this quality is dead. It's important to know what's possible.

The furnace tour continues west of Ashland in Carter County. Two miles north of Grayson is a little community called Pactolus, at the junction of Highways 1 and 7, birthplace of Leonard Sly, better known as Roy Rogers. Pactolus also has a run-down furnace right by the road. This one was a blast furnace that used hydropower from the Little Sandy River. If your interest is piqued, continue north on Highway 7 to the ruins of Iron Hill Furnace, once the largest charcoal-powered blast furnace in the region. Stay on Highway 7 until it merges with Highway 2, then continue to Highway 1773, turn left (west) and go 4 miles to Boone Furnace on Grassy Creek; this blast furnace was built by Sebastian Eifort and started producing iron in 1857.

South of Grayson is the **Mount Savage Furnace,** one of the best preserved and most beautifully made furnaces in the state. If you only want to see one furnace, this is the judges' choice. Take Highway 7 south of Grayson, and turn east on Highway 773. The

Mount Savage Furnace

furnace is on the left, about 1½ miles east of Hitchins. The gorgeous stonework was done in 1848 by a Prussian mason named John Fauson.

Carter County is the only county in the state that has two state parks. From Mount Savage, continue south on Highway 7 to the Grayson Lake State Park. It boasts one of the clearest, most serene lakes (1,500 acres!) in the state. The park offers camping, boating, fishing, swimming, and picnicking—all the ingredients necessary for a relaxing, All-American vacation. Call (606) 474–9727 for more information.

The other park is **Carter Caves State Resort Park,** one of the most magnificent in this whole region of the United States. From Grayson, take Interstate 64 or Highway 60 west, and go north on Highway 182. In addition to a lodge, camping facilities, a pool, canoe trips, and hiking trails, there are twenty navigated caves, three of which are lighted for tours. Many of the caves are wild and can be seen only if you're excited by the idea of real spelunking. One of the best times to try your hand (and elbows and knees) at caving is during the park's annual Crawlathon in early February, when the best guided tours are given.

Two of the park's most significant parts are Bat Cave and Cascade Caverns, both of which are State Nature Preserves. Bat Cave is part-time home to one of the nation's largest wintering populations of the Indiana bat, a federally endangered species. The bats hang in tight clusters in cracks and on the ceiling. No winter tours are allowed in this cave because it is important NOT to disturb these creatures during the winter; they have stored just enough fat to keep them alive during hibernation, and flying would use up their reserves. Cascade Caverns is not contiguous with the rest of the park. Take Highway 182 south and turn west onto Highway 209 and follow signs. Above ground on the north slopes by the caverns are some rare plants that are usually found much farther north; a number of shrublike mountain maple trees can be found here along the stream that flows out of the cave toward Tygarts Creek where, by the way, the hemlock forest will take your breath away. Call for information about any facets of Carter Caves Park at (606) 286–4411 or (800) 325–0059.

While driving from Carter Caves to Cascade Caverns, watch for the Northeastern Kentucky Museum and Gift Shop. From March through October, 9:00 A.M. to 5:00 P.M., seven days a week, you can take a visual crash course in regional history beginning with ancient Indian artifacts, to pioneer times, Civil War through World War II, and into the present. If you're visiting in the winter and want to tour the museum, make an appointment with Jim Plummer at (606) 286–6012.

Morehead is a typical university town in that it's plopped right down in the hills of eastern Kentucky. A friend of mine chose to go to Morehead State because he loves to rock climb and sail, two sports hard to pursue at most Kentucky colleges. Sailing and all other forms of boating and water play are available at 8,270-acre Cave Run Lake, fed by the Licking River. If you're interested in learning about how such massive bodies of water are formed and maintained, arrange a tour of the Corps of Engineers dam and towers by calling (606) 784–9709. If you want a less technical view, dive in. Fishing may be the most popular thing to do at Cave Run. In fact, it's becoming known as the "Muskie Capital of the World." For information on fishing, camping, or anything concerning the lake, call the Morehead Tourist Commission at (606) 784–6221.

The **Morehead State University Folk Art Collection,** on campus in the Claypool-Young Art Building, is outstanding. In addition to rotating exhibits of works by contemporary artists, it includes a delightful collection of decorated gourds, quilts, wood carvings, paintings, sculpture baskets, handmade musical instruments, and handmade tools, all of which have been determined to be folk art. By some definitions, folk art is comprised of objects that are part of everyday life and that somehow reflect the beliefs, social structure, and experiences of the people in a given region; training in the art or craft is usually not received outside the culture from which it springs. You'll understand when you see this impressive little collection. You'll also find yourself thinking deeply and laughing your head off—great responses to art of any kind.

This gallery is even more unusual because it features an artist-in-residence—"Granny Toothman," spinner and weaver extraordinaire. If you think you recognize Lyndall Toothman (her real name), it may be that you saw her in one of Eliot Wigginton's Foxfire books about the folkways of Appalachia. Or, perhaps you were in women's prison in Alderson, West Virginia, in the 1940s where she ran a weaving program. Some of the prisoners she met included such infamous ladies as Ma Barker, Tokyo Rose, and Mrs. Machine Gun Kelly.

Although she'll spin almost anything, Granny Toothman is primarily known for spinning and weaving dog hair, something she's been doing since the 1960s. You'll be impressed by the fine quality of a dog-hair coat or handbag. Gallery hours are Monday through Friday, 8:00 A.M. to 4:00 P.M. during the academic year. Call (606) 783–2760 for more information.

In downtown Morehead, Bishop's Drug Store on Main Street has been open since 1896. You can sit on one of the ten counter stools and have a good old banana split, a real milk shake, fresh lemonade or orangeade, and cherry or chocolate Cokes. The clincher is that a small Coca-Cola, after all these years, only costs five cents, a price that owner, Robert Bishop, does not plan to raise as long as he's the boss.

Down at the bottom tip of Cave Run Lake, where the Licking River begins to look like a river again, is the town of West Liberty, the Morgan County Seat. Come to town the last weekend in September for the Morgan County Sorghum Festival. In the evenings people around here put on their dancing shoes. During the day someone always sets up a mule-drawn sugar cane mill at the Old Mill Park on the banks of the Licking River so you can see how sorghum molasses is made the old-fashioned way. Call Ethel Phillips at (606) 743–3695 or 743–3648.

Off the Beaten Path in Northern Kentucky

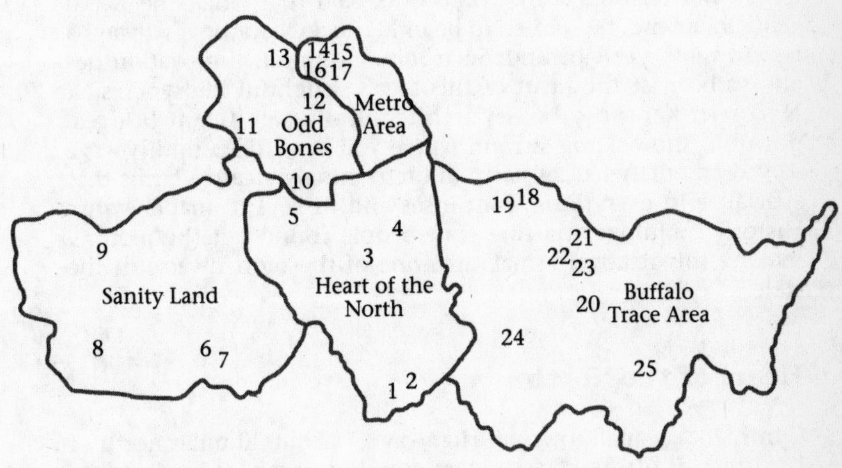

1. Seldon Renaker Inn
2. Wyle Wynde Nursery and Iris Garden
3. Sugar Bush Farm
4. Kincaid Regional Theatre
5. The Quilt Box
6. Jubilee Candle Shop
7. Larkspur Press
8. Clements' Garage
9. Ski Butler
10. Lloyd Wildlife Area
11. Big Bone Lick
12. Tewes Poultry Farm
13. Anderson Ferry
14. Cathedral Basilica of the Assumption
15. Mimosa Mansion
16. Sandford House Bed and Breakfast
17. The Village Puppet Theatre
18. The Beehive Tavern
19. The Lamplighter Inn
20. Jenny's Doll House Museum
21. Joseph Byrd Brannen & Co.
22. Washington
23. Brodrick's Tavern Food & Spirits
24. Blue Licks Battlefield State Park
25. Goddard (White) Covered Bridge

Northern Kentucky

Like some of its most fascinating inhabitants, northern Kentucky is a bit eccentric. Places to explore range from exquisite Gothic cathedrals and puppet theaters in dense urban areas to anachronistic service stations and prehistoric museums in sparsely populated rural regions. Mark Twain once said that when the world came to an end, he wanted to be in Kentucky because it's always a good twenty years behind. Such misconceptions! Innovation has always been at the heart of this area's delightful idiosyncrasies. Northern Kentucky boasts architecturally significant bridges, downhill snow-skiing, an inn where you can't sleep until you've solved an entangled mystery, and refreshingly creative farms that specialize in everything from irises and turkeys to maple syrup. Historic buildings and fine craftspeople round out the picture, making this relatively small area one of the most diverse in the state.

Heart of the North

Cynthiana, a small town on Highway 27 about 30 miles north of Lexington, offers classy overnight lodging at **The Seldon Renaker Inn** at 24 South Walnut Street. Go downtown, turn right on Pleasant Street, right again onto Walnut Street, and watch for the sign on the right. The inn is in a graceful, Victorian house, built as a residence by Seldon Renaker in 1885 and later used as a boarding house, dress shop, tea room, and doctor's office. Room rates are $40 per night. In the morning coffee and doughnuts or coffee cake are available in the first floor communal parlor. For reservations call (606) 234–5756; after 5:00 P.M. call (606) 234–3240 or 234–3554.

Wyle Wynde Nursery and Iris Garden is a painter's paradise and a gardener's endless shopping spree. In mid-May the rows and rows of bearded iris on the nursery's hillside explode into mind-boggling color variations and a sweet, subtle, canteloupelike aroma fills the air. The scene when you crest the hill about 6 miles east of Cynthiana on Highway 62 is breathtaking. Grab your wallet and take a leisurely walk around six acres of beds filled to capacity with irises and other ornamental plants.

Owner-gardeners Norvel and Rita Glascock do their own

hybridizing. The result is a shocking variety of plants like the large "Starburst" iris in lush autumn colors, or "Caesar's Brother," a tall elegant plant with small, blackish-purple blooms. Plants are dug after bloom season and shipped in July. Daylilies are shipped later. For a catalog, write the Glascocks at Wyle Wynde Nursery, U.S. 62, Cynthiana, KY 41031. The nursery is open to the public from late April to mid-June, 10:00 A.M. to 6:00 P.M., Tuesday through Saturday, and 1:00 to 6:00 P.M. on Sundays. You can also call (606) 234–3879.

The most delectable maple syrup south of the Mason-Dixon comes from the steep woods of **Sugar Bush Farm** where the two best kinds of maple, Sugar Maple (*Acer saccarum*) and Black Maple (*Acer nigrum*), grow abundantly. Robert Aulick and the Haubner family have rigged a spider's weblike pipeline system that links three groups of 200 tapped trees and runs the sap downhill to the bottomland near Fork Lick Creek and into old milk tanks. In late winter and early spring, the sap is hauled twice a day to a tobacco barn and pumped into overhead tanks that feed into the wood-fired evaporator. The sap is boiled at around 220 degrees Fahrenheit, and liquid gold flows into the small finishing tanks where it is admired by the alchemists before they strain and can it for the world's pleasure. It takes thirty-five to forty-five gallons of sap to make one gallon of syrup. Eat it over fresh yogurt or hot pancakes, and you will be eating like a god.

You can find the Sugar Bush Farm folks every year at Pendleton County's Wool Festival, held in the Falmouth fairgrounds on Highway 27, the first weekend of October. Call (606) 654–3406 for details. You are also welcome to go directly to the farm to meet these delightful folks in their own setting. To get there from Highway 25, which runs parallel to Interstate 75, go to Williamstown and take Highway 22 east out of town about 5 miles. Turn south on Highway 1054, again for about 5 miles, and look for a green sign that says SUGAR BUSH FARM at the entrance to Jenkins Road. Turn right and go all the way to the end of the road. It's best to call ahead if you want to visit (606) 654–3433.

Thaxton's South Fork Canoe Trails, Inc. offers year-round canoe trips on the Main Licking River, the South Fork, and the Middle Fork. Seeing the countryside by its natural roadways can connect one to the land in a way that driving a car cannot. No road noise. No cursing at your fellow human beings for passing on a hill. Nothing between your skin and the living world. In Falmouth on

Highway 330 near its juncture with Highway 27, you'll see signs for the base livery. Farther north on Highway 27, the Main Licking Outpost is near a bridge in Butler. Call (606) 472–2000 for more information.

In the 200-year-old town of Falmouth, the most notable well-preserved historic building is a handsome two-story log cabin, circa 1790, called the Alvin Mountjoy House on Chapel Street, which runs parallel to Main Street downtown. In addition to the traditional walls of huge poplar logs, pine floors, and big fireplaces built of stone from the nearby Licking River, it is one of the few existing eighteenth-century cabins that have basements. The present-day owners, Carol and Nancy Houchen, open the building on weekdays from 9:00 A.M. to 2:00 P.M.

The **Kincaid Regional Theatre** is a small, professional summer theater that features new shows every season. From mid-June through the end of July you can see Broadway musicals in the Falmouth Auditorium. In downtown Falmouth, go east on Shelby Street, then south on Chapel Street and look for signs. Curtain time is 8:15 P.M., Thursday through Saturday, and 2:30 P.M. on Sunday. Dinner packages are available. For reservations or a performance schedule, write KRT, Route 5, Box 225, Falmouth, KY 41040, or call (606) 654–6911 or 654–2636.

Every quilter I know harbors a special kind of gratitude for **The Quilt Box,** one of the largest and most comprehensive quilt shops in the state. When I first laid eyes on Charlotte Willis's marvelous quilt, "Kentucky Pride," my first question was "Where did she find such gorgeous materials?" This little shop has them. Natalie Lahner and her daughter Darcy Koenig have made it their mission to carry every quilt-related item imaginable, including more than 1,500 bolts of 100 percent cotton fabric in colors and patterns that look good enough to eat, patterns, notions, books, and, of course, actual quilts. They make custom quilts based on wallpaper or upholstery samples or unusual designs.

The store is in a restored 150-year-old log structure tastefully married to the Lahners' residence, a reproduction seventeenth-century house. Kids love seeing the rabbits, chickens, sheep, ducks, miniature horses, or whatever current farm residents are on the loose. From Interstate 75, take the Dry Ridge Owenton (Exit 159) and go west on Highway 22. Turn right on Highway 467 (Warsaw Road), go exactly 2⁶⁄₁₀ miles and look for the Walnut Springs Farm mailbox and the sign for THE QUILT BOX. Follow the gravel road $\frac{4}{10}$ mile to the only house on the road. Call (606) 824–4007.

All year, every day from 6:00 A.M. to 10:00 P.M., the Country Grill at 21 Taft Highway in Dry Ridge serves consistently good-n-good-for-you meals made from fresh ingredients. The phone number is (606) 824–6000. It's a good sign when the parking lot is always full.

Sanity Land

A few miles south of Owenton on Highway 127 sits a pink frame house on a hill in a yard full of angular alligators and stylized wide-eyed beasts. This is not a cubist zoo, but Siegel Pottery. Although Greg Siegel has a reputation for producing clay reptiles, he also makes a variety of functional pots, but not without some humor. For example, a big, sturdy dinner plate glazed with a long pink spiral surrounded by blue comma-shaped dots is called "Boys and Girl." All of the pieces are made of stoneware clay and high-fired to about 2,400 degrees Fahrenheit. Many of the sculptural pieces are decorated with local clays and fired in a salt kiln, which produces a rich, earthy effect. The Siegels work at home, so hours are by chance. Rebekka Siegel makes exquisite modern quilts. If you have a serious love for this art, ask to see a few of her favorites, or whatever is in progress. She also teaches seminars in quilt technique and design. You can reach the Siegels at (502) 484–2970.

About 10 miles south of Owenton on Highway 127, the little town of Monterey has a few pleasant surprises. In town right next to the highway is the **Jubilee Candle Shop** (502–484–5760). The owner, Paula Nye, has dominated the handmade candle scene in Kentucky since the mid-1970s. Her style is distinctive—bold colors and all imaginable shapes. Stop in the studio and see how art candles are made. Next door is a new craft shop full of locally made works. Ask here about arts events like literary readings, concerts, and dances held every so often at the Monterey Volunteer Fire Department.

Also in downtown Monterey is **Larkspur Press,** a fine little press that is Gray Zeitz's pride and joy. Larkspur books, primarily small chapbooks or broadsides by Kentucky writers, are of high quality in form and in content. All productions are done in letterpress from type set by hand and printed on paper that makes you want to touch and linger. Visitors are welcome, but call ahead, because the press may be moving and Zeitz keeps odd hours; the phone number is (502) 484–5390.

Leave Monterey and go south on Highway 561, then take Highway 573 northwest for about 12 miles to New Castle. From downtown New Castle turn south onto Highway 421 to **Clements' Garage,** a Chevron station with a sign over the garage door that reads HOME SERVICE STATION. In the office you'll find that it is a kind of home for the owner, Katie Clements (born in 1905) and her "young helpers," Henry and Earl, both over sixty. She sits by the cozy oil stove and quilts while her seventeen parakeets chatter insanely by the door. A big red 5-cent Coca-Cola cooler is full of drinks and still chugging along, just like the station's 1951 Chevy truck and Katie's 1950 four-door sedan. Earl will be glad to show you shelves full of dust-covered, brand-new spark plugs, belts, and radiator caps for Model T's and A's. Old car buffs, take note: Katie would like "to get shed of all them old things." Clements' garage still sells gas, select antiques, and they'll fix anything on a car. So no matter what you're driving, come in next time you're in New Castle, you hear?

To get to Port Royal, go north on Highway 421 a little way, then veer onto Highway 193 and go a right smart piece. When asking directions in Kentucky, you need to understand how far "a piece" is. Unfortunately, I can't give you an absolute definition. "Just a little piece" can mean a couple of miles or a few hundred yards, depending on the look in a person's eyes and the tone of voice. If you don't imply, by your demeanor, that you will believe the directions, the direction-giver may as well lie . . . and might. A body can travel "a little piece" without completely running dry on patience. Private polling tells me "a little piece" is equivalent to "two whoops and a holler." "A far piece" is as far as language permits us to discuss distance and is, in fact, unattainable. "A right smart piece" is pretty far, but you can get there. And, finally, you must be warned about "no piece at all" or it will fool you all your life, because it sounds like you're already there, but it's farther than that. Allen M. Trout defined it this way: "Say you take a chew of tobacco when you start. When you have walked far enough to have chewed and spit all the flavor out, you have come 'no piece at all.' " Those who abstain from tobacco use will surely be lost.

There is nothing to see in Port Royal but the land and the people who live by the land. That's all there is to see in many other areas of the state, but I'd like for those who are familiar with writer, teacher, and farmer, Wendell Berry, to take a good look at northern Henry County where he makes his home. The Kentucky River forms the eastern border of the county. Here the river basin is wide, the flat bottomland soil rich, the steep hills wooded and deserted. This varied terrain insists that it be farmed in various ways. Except in the wide river bottomland, the arable areas are limited to small, odd-shaped patches that Wendell Berry chooses to farm with a team of draft horses.

One of the truths he repeats is that finicky areas like these are not unique to Henry County. The idiosyncrasies of all lands must be intimately and humbly understood before we can live on them as responsible stewards. We talk of preserving the wilderness, but we don't preserve the farmland from which we feed ourselves. Farmers are, after all, people who use nature directly, not only for themselves, but also for consumers, by proxy. Wherever you live and travel, look at the land and think about the mystery of your dependency on nature and about how you, in turn, can respond responsibly. Don't try this alone—talk to people and read Wendell Berry's work.

From Port Royal, follow Highway 389 north into Carroll County, through the town of English, where there are ramps onto Interstate 71, and into Carrollton. Despite popular opinion nationwide, snow skiing in Kentucky is not an oxymoron. It's true that **Ski Butler,** in the General Butler State Resort Park, often has to make snow, but the trails are considered safe and challenging. Skiing and snowboarding are available from mid-December through February. For park information and specific hours, call (502) 732–4231. For a ski report, call (502) 732–8767.

Downtown Carrollton boasts two unusual places of lodging. The P. T. Baker Bed and Breakfast House at 406 Highland Avenue is cozy and serves breakfast at the hour of your choosing. For reservations, call (502) 732–4210 on weekends; on weekdays call (606) 525–7088. The Carrollton Inn at 218 Main Street is a restored 1812 Colonial inn with ten rooms and a full dining room and lounge. The phone number is (502) 732–6905.

Just upriver a few miles is Warsaw, a peaceful one-traffic-light rivertown in the smallest county in Kentucky. The Gallatin County Historical Society has restored and furnished an 1843 Gothic Revival–style home. Follow Interstate 75 to Interstate 71

West and take the Warsaw exit. In town, turn right by the courthouse (the second oldest continuously operating courthouse in the state, circa 1837) at the only stoplight and look behind the funeral home for the Hawkins-Kirby House. For a tour, call the local historian, Dr. Carl Bogardus, at (606) 567–4591.

Odd Bones

Eccentricity saves lives. (How's that for a bumper sticker?) The little-known Curtis Gates **Lloyd Wildlife Area** would not exist if the eccentric Mr. Lloyd had not written a twenty-four-page will and testament that outlined in every detail the future management plan for his 365-acre farm. Before he died in 1923, Lloyd erected an enormous granite monument to himself in the woods. One side reads: "Curtis G. Lloyd Born 1859—Died 60 or more years afterwards. The exact number of years, months, and days that he lived nobody knows and nobody cares." The other side says: "Curtis G. Lloyd Monument erected in 1922 by himself for himself during his life to gratify his own vanity. What Fools These Mortals Be!" A fool? Not quite. His preserve boasts one of the shamefully few stands of virgin timber in Kentucky. A forest teeming with wildlife and wilderness left to its own beautiful accord—a black walnut, 36 inches in diameter, towers over acres and acres of huge red oaks and poplars. To think that Interstate 75 is within earshot. . . . From Crittenden, follow Highway 25 south a few miles and look for the sign.

Big Bone Lick is probably the only prehistoric graveyard you'll ever lay eyes on. From Florence, take Highway 127 south (through Sugartit) and turn west on Highway 338 (Beaver Road) at Beaverlick to the town of Big Bone and follow signs to the state park. Probably during the end of the Ice Age (more than 10,000 years ago) many of the largest mammals on the continent who came to this area to lick the rich veins of salt and sulphur died, leaving their bones scattered around the massive mineral deposit. Some of the bones have been identified as belonging to the huge ground sloths, tapirs, musk oxen, giant bison, and deer-like animals called cervalces, all now extinct. No one knows exactly the cause of the worldwide destruction of these species. Some scientists say that glacier expansion drove animals south and created an overly dense population that eventually starved.

Others blame an epidemic, unscrupulous primitive hunters, or the hand of a god.

The salt lick was also used by Native Americans and, after 1729, by pioneers who boiled down the brines to make highly valued salt. Legend has it that early Virginian settlers who were fascinated with the massive bones used mastodon ribs for tent poles and vertebrae for stools. Even Thomas Jefferson was intrigued. He had more than 300 specimens brought to the White House for research, but a servant pounded them into fertilizer. Not all of the bones are lost, however—Big Bone Lick State Park's museum houses an incredible collection of vertebrate fossils from the area. Hours vary throughout the year. Call (606) 384–3522 for information.

Although thousands of people on Interstate 75 see the sign on the side of the barn daily, **Tewes Poultry Farm** is off the beaten path in spirit. The Tewes family (pronounced TOO-wis) raises and processes more than 5,000 turkeys annually and more than 600 chickens every two weeks, in addition to keeping Leghorn hens that lay at least 5,000 eggs a week. Poultry isn't everything, though. Mary Tewes, the head of the 175-acre farm, is the proud mother of 18, grandmother of 72, and great-grandmother of 3. After almost a half-century on the place, she still makes meals on a big wood cookstove, works alongside the younger generations sorting and washing eggs, tends to customers, and does the hundreds of tasks necessary on a "small" farm.

Way before the Interstate existed, the Teweses made final payments on their land by selling Easter chicks dipped in pastel-colored food dyes. Today Interstate 75 cuts through the front pasture, a lumberyard sits adjacent to the house, and planes rush overhead to the Greater Cincinnati International Airport. Easter chicks would barely pay the feed bills. Despite the changes, the Teweses carry on a diverse, wholesome operation. Stop to get fresh fryers, big-breasted roasters, turkeys, bacon, eggs, and a vitamin-like dose of friendliness. Tewes Poultry Farm is just north of Florence. From Interstate 75, take the Buttermilk Pike exit and go into Crescent Springs. Turn left on Anderson Road and look for the farm on the left. They're always home and you're always welcome. The phone number is (606) 341–8844.

Said to be "the world's smallest house of worship," the Monte Casino Chapel measures in at 6 by 9 feet—no better place for an intimate conversation with God. Just close the door and let fly.

The chapel was built in 1810 in a vineyard on a hill outside of Covington by Benedictine monks. In the late 1960s the chapel was moved to its present site on the campus of Thomas More College. From Interstate 75, take Interstate 275 east and exit on Turkeyfoot Road. Monte Casino is next to a large pond on the left side of the road.

If you take the Buttermilk Pike exit and cross to the east side of the Interstate, you won't miss the Oldenberg Brewery and Entertainment Complex. This place is a stereotypical tourist trap, but it is somewhat redeemed by being the only microbrewery in the state. They have hired a German brewmaster to make "limited edition" special beers on site. Tours are available of the brewery and the "World's largest beer memorabilia collection." A pub-style restaurant serves lunch and dinner; Tuesday through Saturday brings live entertainment. Call (606) 341–2804.

Head toward the river, get on Highway 8, follow it west into Constance, and look for the **Anderson Ferry,** a two-boat operation that has been in business since 1817. Today this is the quickest crossing from Cincinnati, via Ohio's Highway 50, to the airport on Interstate 275, especially when the bridges nearer town are choked by rush hour. Paul Anderson's two ferries, Boone 7 (circa 1937) and Boone 8 (or Little Boone), haul passengers on demand year-round. On the Kentucky landing an old character named Arnold hangs out and "treats" customers to an endless, pseudo-history of the boats and his life. From November through April, hours are 6:00 A.M. to 8:00 P.M., and from May through October, from 6:00 A.M. to 9:30 P.M. On Sundays, they start running at 7:00 A.M. Cars are charged $2, trucks $2 and up, and foot passengers are $.25.

Metro Area

If Covington's **Cathedral Basilica of the Assumption** at the corner of Twelfth and Madison streets (606–431–2060) were in a major coastal city or in Europe, people would rave about it. As it is, this remarkable work of French-Gothic architecture is little known to the world. The building is closely modeled after Paris's Notre Dame and the Abbey Church of Saint Denis, complete with flying buttresses and fantastic gargoyles perched high on the front facade. Glass is everywhere. Eighty-two windows, including two

Cathedral Basilica of the Assumption

enormous rose windows, glow endlessly with the changing sun. Measuring 24 feet by 67 feet, the hand-blown, stained glass window in the transept is said to be the largest in the world. The amplitude of rich color and the variety of shapes and expressive details can leave you staggering and dizzy in the huge chamber. In one chapel are several paintings by Frank Duveneck, a Covington native who became an internationally known portrait and genre painter and sculptor. My favorite is the austere center panel of the Eucharist triptych of Mary Magdalene at the foot of the cross. To the visual strength of the space, add the music of three massive pipe organs, and you will be transported. (The basic building was constructed, beginning in 1894, for the price of $150,000, the cost of many of today's middle-American homes.)

The altar in The Blessed Sacrament Chapel reads "Behold the Bread of Angels Becomes the Food of Wayfarers," so the faith-inspired beauty of this temple of worship is available to us worldly wanderers. The basilica is open daily from 8:00 A.M. to 4:30 P.M.

Mutter Gottes Kirch on the corner of West Sixth and Montgomery streets is another of Covington's fabulous churches that is open to visitors. Started in 1870, Mother of God Church was built in Italian (rather than French) Renaissance basilica design. Clock-bearing twin spires over the front facade seem to be held in place by the large apse dome. Inside, the lower level of magnificent stained glass windows depict Old Testament promises while the upper panels depict the corresponding fulfillments. Other inspirational art includes sculpture, some by Covington artist Ferdinand Muer; Stations of the Cross; an 1876 Koehnken and Grimm pipe organ; beautiful floor tile; and large frescoes and murals by Johann Schmitt, who was once Frank Duveneck's teacher and whose work is in the Vatican.

Go through Covington's Licking Riverside Historic District on the east side of town by "the Point" where the Licking River empties into the mighty Ohio. Follow Second Street east until it becomes Shelby Street and wraps around to become Riverside Drive. On the strip of land between the street and the river is the George Rogers Clark Park, named so because Clark supposedly stopped at the site to gather forces on his way to Ohio to fight Shawnees. In the park are a few new pieces of sculpture by George Danhires. The most fun is a bronze likeness of James Bradley, an African-born slave who worked his way to freedom, crossed the Ohio River, attended seminary in Cincinnati in 1834, and went down in history as the only ex-slave to participate in the famous, fiery Lane Seminary debates on abolition. Bradley is depicted as reading thoughtfully on a park bench facing the river. The piece is so realistic that passersby stop talking so as not to disturb the man.

Across the street the Charleston-like houses seem self-conscious, built to be worthy of facing the river. **Mimosa Mansion** at 412 East Second Street is the only building in the area open to the public. Built in 1853–55 by Thomas Porter, Mimosa Mansion is said to be the largest single-family home in all of northern Kentucky. Touring the mansion you experience the original gas lighting system and the first electric system with its carbon filament light bulbs. From January through November hours are Saturday and Sunday, 1:00 to 6:00 P.M.; during December, special Christmas tours are given on weekends from 1:00 to 8:00 P.M. or by appointment. Admission is $3. The phone number is (606) 261–9000.

The bright blue Covington/Cincinnati Suspension Bridge, a few blocks west of the Licking Riverside Neighborhood, was recently renamed The John A. Roebling Suspension Bridge in honor of the engineer who designed it. When it opened in 1867 after twenty-two years of construction, the bridge was the longest of its kind in the world (1,057 feet) and served Roebling as a prototype for his later Brooklyn Bridge in New York City. So what if we weren't the first to have acid-washed designer jeans—Kentucky has bridges.

Take Garrard Street south and look on the right for The Amos Shinkle Townhouse, circa 1877. What was once a posh residence for one of Covington's early big businessmen, Amos Shinkle, is now an impressive bed and breakfast facility. Bernie Moorman, host and owner, has taken pains to maintain such interesting features as the original murals on the walls of the front staircase. Rooms range from a master suite with a whirlpool to sleeping rooms for children in converted carriage-house stalls. Prices range from $62 to $98 per night and include a full breakfast. Call (606) 431–2118 for reservations.

Another handsome place of lodging is the **Sandford House Bed and Breakfast** on 1026 Russell Street in an area known as the Old Seminary Square Historic District (from Eighth to Eleventh streets). Built in the early 1820s for politician Thomas Sandford and sold in 1835 to the Western Baptist Theological Institute, the house was caught in the middle of one of Kentucky's hottest disputes. Northern and Southern trustees feuded so severely over the slavery issue that the seminary was forced to split into two separate schools, one in Georgetown and one in Louisville. Hosts Dan and Linda Carter keep an award-winning garden and serve breakfast in the grand dining room where finishing-school girls ate in the 1890s. Prices begin at $55 a night. Call (606) 291–9133 for reservations.

Although Main Strasse has been billed as a miniature German village in downtown Covington, historically the area is ethnically heterogeneous. In addition to German families, Irish and African Americans have lived in this architecturally fascinating neighborhood that now has been developed into a shopping district for tourists. You can find anything from antiques and doll boutiques to restaurants and bakeries. At the edges of the developed area are local pubs with Irish names.

One of the best restaurants in town is not German, but Cajun. Dee Felice Café at 529 Main Street, next to the Goose Girl Fountain, is hot. The food is spicy, and the jazz is cool. From a $3 bowl of gumbo to a $19 blackened salmon, the flavor tugs at the southern palate. It's hard to believe that the ornate building was originally a pharmacy. No Super-X can hold a candle to these pressed-tin ceilings and miniature Corinthian columns, preserved in the restaurant and painted in audacious colors. Tuesday through Sunday nights a live band made up of local musicians plays Dixieland, blues, and lots of jazz on a stage behind the long bar. Owner Dee Felice is a jazz drummer in his own right. Rumor has it he used to play with James Brown. Lunch hours are 11:00 A.M. to 3:00 P.M. Dinner begins at 5:00 P.M. nightly. Call (606) 261–2373 for more information.

On the beaten path of Main Strasse, but worth your time if you have young children, is **The Village Puppet Theatre** at 606 Main Street. Owner and master puppeteer Charles Killian advertises "good clean fun . . . with strings attached." Year-round, Tuesday through Sunday, "live" puppet shows are performed during the day. Great traditional stories like "Jack and the Beanstalk" and "The Elves and the Shoemaker" are scheduled along with musical shows featuring trick marionettes. The lobby has a concession stand and a small store featuring, of course, puppets ranging from inexpensive hand puppets to giant, intricate marionettes. Tickets are $5 for adults, $4 for children. Hours are 9:00 A.M. to 5:00 P.M. on Tuesday through Thursday; noon to 8:00 P.M. on Friday; and noon to 4:00 P.M. on Saturday and Sunday. Call for exact showtimes at (606) 291–5566.

Iron Horse history buffs, take note of the Railway Exposition Company, Inc., Museum at 315 West Southern Avenue. This museum has a number of immaculately preserved items like a 1906 Southern RR open platform business car, a diner built for The Golden Rocket, several locomotives, sleeping cars, post office cars, cabooses, and more. Guided tours of the museum are available from May through October on Saturdays, Sundays, and holidays from 1:00 to 4:00 P.M. Admission is charged. Call (606) 491–RAIL for more information.

Across the Licking River and northeast of Newport is the Weller Haus Bed and Breakfast in Bellevue's Taylor Daughters' Historic District at 319 Poplar Street (two blocks south of Highway 8). For $50 to $60, you can eat a classy breakfast and sleep peacefully amidst eighteenth-century antiques in an attractive, folk-style Victorian house. Call (606) 431–6829 for reservations.

Buffalo Trace Area

The river towns strung along the mighty Ohio and the areas that spread away from them are usually historically significant, and, for that reason, often a touch schizophrenic, caught between the stillness of the past and the fluid present. Augusta, in Bracken County, is one of the few such towns that has struck a happy balance while remaining scenic. From Covington/Newport, either hug the banks of the Ohio River by following Highway 8 east, or buzz along the brand-new "AA" Highway 546, which connects Alexandria and Ashland. Both highways lead to Augusta. If you take the "AA," watch for its intersection with Highway 1159. Turn left (north) and meander around for a moment at the Walcott Covered Bridge, a 75-foot wooden bridge spanning Locust Creek, active from 1824 until 1954. Walk into the bridge and read the descriptions of bridge types, definitions of terms, and explanations for methods of construction.

You may have already seen Augusta if you watched the T.V. miniseries "Centennial." The town was used to film scenes taking place in St. Louis, Missouri, in the 1880s. Because Augusta has no flood wall, Water Street (or Riverside Drive) was a ready-made set, except for a few details—the film crew put down 4 inches of dirt on the street to cover the pavement and pulled down power lines and business signs. The houses along the river were, as they always are, picture perfect. Since then, several Public Broadcasting Systems (PBS) productions have been filmed in Augusta, including the classic "Huckleberry Finn."

The Beehive Tavern on the north corner of Main Street and Riverside Drive is an elegant Colonial-style restaurant in a 1970s row house facing the river. Drinks are served from noon until closing on Wednesday through Saturday on the upstairs balcony, which has a perfect river view. Inside, lunch and dinner are served from noon to 8:00 P.M. on Wednesday and Thursday, from noon to 9:00 P.M. on Friday and Saturday, and from 1:00 to 7:00 P.M. on Sunday. The menu ranges from simple favorites like black bean soup for $2.50 to roast pork with fried apples for $11.50, and desserts are primo—blueberry trifle cake or caramel flan. Call Luciano Moral at (606) 756–2202.

Directly across the street is the Augusta Ferry, one of the very few functional ferries on the Ohio River. It's operational year-round during daylight hours, and although a trip schedule exists, the captain will carry you across any time. Imagine yourself crossing the water when the town was new and the ferry was powered by mules. One block east of the ferry is the Riverside House 1860 Bed and Breakfast, a meticulously renovated Victorian home. For $72 a night you get the full Victorian treatment—bedrooms decked-out in period antiques, English breakfast, high tea at 4:00 P.M., and one of the most serene views of the river in town. Call (606) 756–2458 for reservations.

One of the most innovative, zany businesses in the entire state of Kentucky is **The Lamplighter Inn** at 103 West Second Street in downtown Augusta. If you want lodgings, they are here. But if you're ready to walk into a full-fledged Agatha Christie–like mystery, plan to come for a Saturday night and invite your friends—the Tongret family, owners and master-schemers, facilitate a mystery whenever at least five rooms are reserved.

Alan C. Tongret, actor, writer, and son of the proprietors Charles and Doris Tongret, writes and produces all of the mysteries for the inn. One of the favorites to date is "The Red Stockings—Spitballs Caper," a mystery involving a baseball game, a bag of gold, two murders, fiction, and truth. The guests get their first clues in the early afternoon in order to spend the rest of the day and night solving the puzzle. In this mystery more clues come in the form of baseball paraphernalia planted in businesses around town. The guest who solves the mystery first wins a prize, as does the guest who plays the role of murderer. Rates for mystery nights are $144.50 to $159.50 for a double room. This includes dinner with live entertainment, a reception for the mystery, and breakfast in the morning. Call for details and reservations at (606) 756–2603.

A popular event in the area is "The Old Reliable" Germantown Fair, held the first week in August at the Germantown fairgrounds on Highway 10. No one seems to be able to explain the "Old Reliable" aspect beyond the fact that it happens every year. Germantown straddles the Bracken/Mason County line. Thirty-three yards from that county line in Germantown is a classic country-cooking restaurant called Jim's Ole Country Inn. There's nothing particularly German about the place, but fast food can't hold a candle to the speed of the cooks, and you get a real meal to boot. Hours are 7:00 A.M. to 7:00 P.M., Monday to Wednesday; on Sunday it closes at 2:00 P.M.; and every other day it closes at 8:00 P.M.

Follow Highway 8 or the "AA" east to Maysville. If you arrive from the west via Highway 8, take a moment to stop at a functional covered bridge at Dover. Highway 1235 crosses Lee's Creek by means of this 61-foot "Queensport truss" bridge; it once had a toll booth at one end when the oldest part was built in 1835. Maysville is the next town upriver, the site of the closest bridge to the north, and the hub of activity for the whole area. To steep yourself in area history, go to the Mason County Museum (606–564–5865) at 215 Sutton Street in an 1878 structure originally built to be the town's first library. Because of the historic significance of the area as an early point of access to the west, the little museum tells the bigger story of the expansion of America.

The Limestone Square Mall is an indoor mall on Market Street, with an entrance that's easy to miss. Go downhill on the left side of the street and watch for a glass door or enter from around the corner on Second Street. In the mall, Jenny's Doll and Gift Shop has an astounding number of new, high-quality dolls. More than sixty contemporary doll manufacturers are represented on the shelves with figures as varied as Batman's enemy, The Joker, to realistic German-made children with human hair. Sandra Marshall and her young daughter, Jenny, run the business with a passion. They say they'll try to find even the most obscure doll by request, and they ship all over the world.

As is true for most of us, Sandra's passion for dolls began in her childhood. Her interest in dolls remained in the past until recently, when she began buying antique dolls like crazy. Now she has a three-room house in Lewisburg filled with more than 4,500 dolls ranging from one-half-inch in size to life-sized mannequins of children. She has also collected several hundred doll toys of all sizes, and coins, stamps, and bank notes to accompany the foreign dolls. She calls her private collection **Jenny's Doll House Museum,** again in honor of her daughter. This collection is separate from the Maysville shop. Nothing is for sale, but it may be viewed (by appointment only). Because she is in the process of moving to another location, call ahead for directions at (606) 564–6033 or 742–2119.

Follow Second Street past Sutton and park anywhere. On the north corner of Sutton and Wall streets is the shop of a fine furniture maker. **Joseph Byrd Brannen & Co.** Antique Furniture Reproductions is an inspirational one-man operation. Joe Brannen is asked to make all manner of hardwood furniture, but his true love is for traditional eighteenth- and nineteenth-century American furniture in cherry, walnut, mahogany, and curly maple, a wood with delicious figuring and a mean grain from which many woodworkers keep a respectful distance. Joe uses power tools but finishes all of his work by hand using planes or scrapers that are fueled by pure elbow grease. The difference is noticeable and worth the extra cost. He always has a few finished pieces of furniture on hand and welcomes visitors Monday through Saturday from 9:00 A.M. to 5:00 P.M., except on Thursday. For a brochure and price list, write to Joseph Bryd Brannen, 145 West Second Street, Maysville, KY 41056, or call (606) 564–3642.

Directly across the street on the corner is Gantley's Shoe and Harness Repair Shop, another impressive one-craftsperson operation. Joe Gantley can do just about anything with leather. Although he is set up for small work like making belts and repairing shoes and purses, he prefers working on equine equipment. Joe is known all over the state as a fine rider and trainer of five-gaited Saddlebreds. Ask him about the horse show photos in his shop. He's open weekdays during business hours. Call him at (606) 564–9875.

Drive west another two blocks to Rosemary Clooney Street, so named when her first motion picture premiered in Maysville, her hometown. Go toward the river and you'll find the only active Amtrak station in Kentucky and a great place to eat called Caproni's Restaurant. Its national fame began in the 1930s when it was just a café where eastbound soldiers stopped during train layovers. Today, two long balconies look out over a wide, slow-moving part of the Ohio River. The other selling point is super food, high-quality local and foreign wines, and imported beers. You can have the usual range of country cooking done with unusual class, or you can indulge in a savory plate of fettucine Alfredo for a mere $5.95, a New York strip for $12.95, or a variety of seafoods. Call (606) 564–9725.

Driving the 4 miles straight uphill on Highway 68 between Maysville and **Washington** will take you a matter of minutes. In the eighteenth century, however, the climb consumed a whole day. Horses pulling heavily loaded wagons and carts across the Ohio River at Maysville (then called Limestone) were worn out by the time they reached the ridge, so they stopped at Washington for a rest. I wouldn't call these pioneers tourists, but their patronage caused the town to grow from a few humble cabins into a bunch of humble cabins.

The area was settled by Simon Kenton who first claimed the land in the late 1770s. Kenton later sold it for $.50 an acre to Arthur Fox and William Wood, who laid out the town of Washington. Like a good imperialist, Kenton had come to the area in search of sugar cane so that he could get rich making Jamaican-style rum. The hills were indeed covered with cane, but it was wild Kentucky cane, a tall, woody, native grass that is the only bamboo species native to North America. Nothing sweet about it. Like a good capitalist, Kenton realized his error and went on to exploit some other aspect of the land. He eventually opened a small store in a cabin in Washington. Legend has it that Kenton couldn't pay his bills and was thrown into debtor's prison in Washington, the very town he founded. The tables do turn. . . .

When Kentucky joined the Union in 1792, people west of the Alleghenies thought that Washington, population 462, might become the capital of the United States. (Obviously, the other Washington got the vote.) If time could have frozen at that moment, you probably would have seen a town that looked much like the historic restoration that stands today. You can get a more complete story of the town and its characters from one of the tour guides at the Visitors' Center between May 1 and early

December, Monday through Saturday, 10:00 A.M. to 4:40 P.M., and Sunday from 1:00 to 4:00 P.M. Rates are $2 for adults and $1 for students. Call (606) 759–7411 for more information.

Washington is full of small antique and specialty shops selling everything from rare books to homemade candies, clocks, yarns, dried herbs, and copper lamps. The place to eat in town is **Brodrick's Tavern Food & Spirits** (606–759–5225) at the corner of Main and "C" streets. This place has been licensed since 1789 when the first court of the new Mason County, for which Washington served as county seat, granted David Brodrick permission "to keep an ordinary in his home." Those tired hill-climbers rested here before heading down the buffalo trace. Lunch is usually served from 11:30 A.M. to 5:00 P.M. Weekend dinner hours begin at 5:00 P.M.

Highway 68 follows a north-south path made by buffalo traveling to and from the salt deposit at Blue Licks. From Maysville, where the buffalo crossed the river, go south on the Buffalo Trace, as it's called, to the **Blue Licks Battlefield State Park.** The place has always been one of importance to the native people as well as to the settlers who mined salt here. Its connotation darkened when in August of 1792 more than sixty Kentucky pioneers were killed in a bloody Revolutionary battle against Indians and Canadian soldiers ten months *after* the British surrendered at Yorktown—all in a fifteen-minute battle. A large granite obelisk at the park marks the area where the men, including Daniel Boone's son Israel, were buried in a common grave.

Beginning in the parking area, take a hike along the buffalo trace. This fifteen-acre area is set aside as a state nature preserve in order to protect one of the last and largest stands of Short's Goldenrod, a federally endangered species. Notice how the goldenrod grows thickest in the open areas. It is speculated that grazing and trampling by buffalo, now nonexistent in Kentucky, helped the plant to survive; the buffalo may have also carried the seeds in their thick fur and spread the graceful yellow plant. (Goldenrod, by the way, is not responsible for your hay fever. Blame ragweed.) Goldenrod blooms in September, but as tempting as it is, please don't pick any.

The displays in the park museum are concerned with the cultural and geographic history of the area. Several original pieces of Daniel Boone's salt-making equipment are in the museum, donated by descendants of Simon Kenton. In 1778 Boone and a few others made a salt expedition and were taken prisoner by some local natives. Later Simon Kenton retrieved the equipment and thereby managed to preserve it for posterity. Today the park has fishing facilities and all the usual recreational trappings. In mid-August the park sponsors a historic reenactment of the battle during a festival that features period demonstrators and other related entertainment.

The Buffalo Trace area is definitely the region of covered bridges. Johnson Creek Covered Bridge crosses the creek on the original Buffalo Trace north of Blue Licks Park. Built in 1874, the dilapidated structure is 114 feet long and 16 feet wide, with Smith-type trusses. Take Highway 68 east from the park, then take Highway 165 north to Highway 1029 and watch for the bridge, which is closed to traffic.

Another covered bridge of exactly the same length is the Cabin Creek Bridge near Cottageville in Lewis County. This

Covered Bridge

bridge is also dilapidated and closed to traffic. From Maysville, take Highway 10 through Plumville and turn left (east) onto Spring Creek Road. Just as you cross the county line at the intersection with Cabin Road, the bridge is on the south side.

In Fleming County, south of Maysville, you can see three covered bridges. The first is the 60-foot-long **Goddard (White) Covered Bridge,** the only surviving example of Ithiel Town truss design in the state, a latticelike design that uses rigid, triangularly placed beams as supports. Photographers love this spot because a picturesque country church can be seen through the bridge. From Maysville, go to the county seat, Flemingsburg, by way of Highway 11 south. Then follow Highway 32 east almost 6 miles to Goddard. This time you can drive over the bridge. Call (606) 845–5951 for further information.

Follow Highway 32 down the road a piece and turn right (west) on Rawlings Road or north on Highway 1895 (Maxey Flats Road). At Ringos Mills you'll find an 86-foot bridge built in 1867; it was once part of a large nineteenth-century gristmill.

A more utilitarian-style covered bridge is a few miles away near Grange City. The 86-foot-long Hillsboro Bridge is roofed and sided with corrugated tin and the abutments are made of "red stone." The construction is of the burr truss design with multiple king posts. It's a sight! It's also a shame that it's too run-down to use. To get there from Flemingsburg, drive south on Highway 111, pass Hillsboro, and watch the right side of the road. And, if you want to take Highway 11 south toward Mount Sterling, there is yet another old covered bridge near Sherburne, right on the county line.

Off the Beaten Path in South Central Kentucky

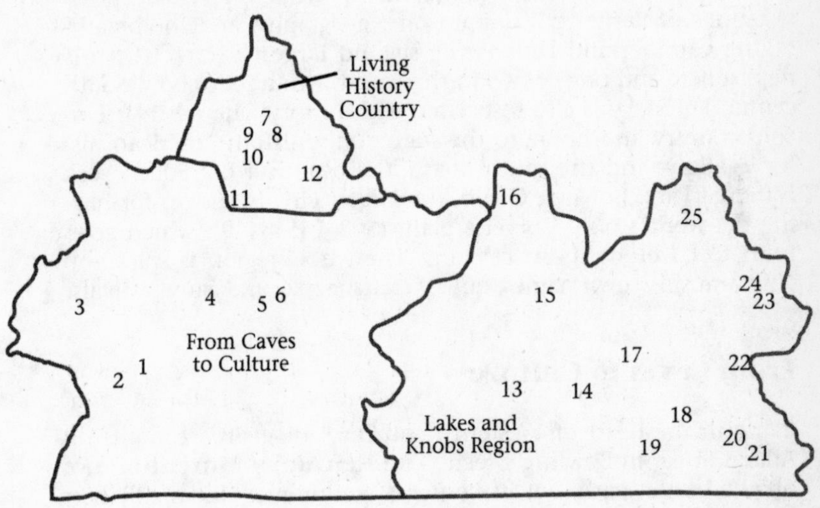

1. The Kentucky Museum
2. The Hobson House
3. Woodbury
4. The Mammoth Cave National Park
5. The American Cave and Karst Center
6. The Horse Cave Theatre
7. Schmidt's Coca-Cola Museum
8. Emma Reno Connor Black History Gallery
9. The Olde Bethlehem Academy Inn
10. The Whistle Stop Restaurant
11. Nolin River Nut Tree Nursery
12. Hodgenville
13. Lake Cumberland
14. Mill Springs Mill
15. Bluegrass Wood and Leather Craft
16. Lou's Leathers
17. Burnside
18. Cumberland Falls
19. Blue Heron mining camp
20. Bailey's Country Store
21. Mulberry Friendship Center
22. Harland Sanders Café & Museum
23. The Levi Jackson State Park
24. Minnie's Gourd-Craft Museum
25. Renfro Valley

South Central Kentucky

Kids aren't the only people who need to play and learn. This region's parks and large man-made lakes are like big playgrounds for adults. Two of the world's natural wonders are in south central Kentucky. Mammoth Cave highlights the most spectacular manifestations of Kentucky's unique karst geography, and the breathtaking Cumberland Falls is the second largest cataract in this hemisphere and one of two in the world with a moonbow. South central Kentucky is also associated with history. The north is Lincoln country and home to the state's only African-American history gallery, and the south boasts the beautiful Big South Fork National Park. Bowling Green, the largest city, is known for having the world's only Corvette plant (502–745–8419), which gives tours to covetous sports car fans. The whole region is spiced-up with amusing town names, quirky craftspeople, and zany festivals.

From Caves to Culture

Being in the heart of Western Kentucky University's campus on Adams Street in Bowling Green, **The Kentucky Museum** is not off the beaten path, but its contents are unique. One of the best collections of objects pertaining to Kentucky history and culture is housed here in one place. They also make a special effort to exhibit fine traveling exhibitions and to put together displays using borrowed objects that would otherwise never be in the public view. Traditional Kentucky quilts are the museum's forte. A seventy-year-old Christmas crazy quilt made of silk hat liners is part of the collection. During the holidays a houseful of relatives were snowbound for several weeks, so instead of flipping on the tube and watching game shows, they made a quilt together. Some are political—the 1850 Henry Clay quilt with his portrait in the middle in crewel work was a presentation piece from Mrs. Henry Clay to the wife of Senator John Jordan Crittenden. Some quilts are downright fascinating, like the dizzying 66,000-piece Spectrum Quilt, rare in that it was made in the 1930s by a *man,* a jeweler who had heard that the work would keep his fingers nimble. The list goes on.

You can't help liking Curiosity Hall, a narrow hall on one side of the museum filled with unusual relics with unusual ties to Kentucky. The oddities include objects like doll heads supposedly used during World War I to transport spy messages, and an item known as a "death crown," a ring of feathers found inside the pillow of a deceased person. Some say that the crown means that the person has gone to heaven. Others say that the feathers form a ring slowly during one's life and when the ring is complete, the time has come to die. A friend told me that this belief was so deeply instilled in her during childhood, that, despite her logical nature, she still beats her pillows every morning to fight fate and destroy the feather ring. After a year of marriage, her husband got irritated enough with the habit to ask why in the tarnation she did it. When she explained, he answered, "That's pathetic, honey. These are foam pillows." Museum hours are 9:30 A.M. to 4:00 P.M., Tuesday through Saturday, and 1:00 to 4:30 P.M. on Sunday. Call (502) 745–2592 for further information.

Another downtown museum is **The Hobson House,** also called Riverview because it overlooks the Barren River. In the late nineteenth century the river was bustling with commerce, and homes facing the river had to be worthy of the attention they received. The Hobsons' magnificent, three-story, brick Italianate mansion has been restored and filled with period antiques. Excellent guided tours are given from 10:00 A.M. until noon and 1:00 to 5:00 P.M., Tuesday through Saturday, and 1:00 to 5:00 P.M. on Sunday. To get there, follow Main Avenue north to the outside of the Victoria Street bypass (Hobson Lane), pass the Delafield School, and watch for the sign. Call (502) 843–5565 for more information.

Mariah's Restaurant (502–842–6878) downtown at 801 State Street is located in Bowling Green's oldest brick house. The southern-style food is very good, and they're famous for their appetizers. (It *is* possible to have decent seafood in landlocked states.) They are open from 11:00 A.M. to 10:00 P.M., Monday through Thursday, and 11:00 A.M. to 11:00 P.M. on Friday and Saturday.

In its heyday **Woodbury** was a busy little town on the Green River at the site of Lock and Dam Number 4. After the log structure, which was finished in 1841, washed away in 1965, the Butler County Historical and Genealogical Society developed Woodbury into a museum complex. An old U.S. Corps of Engineers house has been restored and made into The Green River Museum, a visual history lesson about the riverboat era in Woodbury. The remains of the lock and dam structure are visible from the Museum's big porch. From mid-April through mid-September the museum is open noon to 6:00 P.M., Sunday through Thursday, and noon to 8:00 P.M. on Friday and Saturday. The former lock keeper's home has been transformed into The Woodbury House, a restaurant with a reputation for consistently good country cooking. It is open only on weekends, and reservations are recommended. Call (502) 526–6921 to put your name on the list.

During the last weeks of August a local thespian group performs *The Magic Belle,* a musical about the life of George Henry Dabbs (1882–1967), a Butler County artist, writer, and photographer who recorded the life of a Kentucky river town during the turn of the century. Until recently George Dabbs, Jr., the son of the play's protagonist, played the role of an old man named Uncle Smoat. For performance dates, contact Roger Givens at P.O. Box 219, Morgantown, KY 42261, or call (502) 526–3111. No matter what your map says, there is only one path to Woodbury. From the Green River Parkway, exit into Morgantown on Highway 231 and find Highway 403 to Woodbury. If you are coming from Bowling Green, *do not* take Highway 185 north to 263. It's a long drive to a dead-end—the ferry is closed.

Follow Highway 31W south from Bowling Green through Franklin to the Dueling Grounds Race Course (502–586–7778) near Interstate 65. This is a relatively new course where an international steeplechase with a sizable purse is held at least once a year, usually in April. The area is called "Dueling Grounds" because dueling was forbidden in Tennessee but legal in Kentucky in the nineteenth century. Men would go across the border to settle their disputes in a "manly" manner. These days when people take the Bar Association oath (or the gubernatorial oath) in Kentucky, they swear not to engage in dueling.

Notice on your map how the Kentucky border bulges a bit to the south in this area. Legend has it that when the border was surveyed and this land was to be relegated to Tennessee, a farmer named Sanford Duncan invited the surveying team to a party at The Duncan Tavern, a popular spot for travelers on the Louisville/Nashville trek because of the fine food and Kentucky liquor served there. The surveyors were so appreciative (and drunk) that they agreed to survey all of Duncan's land into Kentucky. The heck with straight lines.

If you travel northeast of Bowling Green, you will be in some of the most spectacular cave country in the world. Second to the Kentucky Derby, **The Mammoth Cave National Park** is the best nationally known tourist attraction in the state, and for that reason travelers can get information about cave history and trips anywhere within a hundred-mile radius. When you request cave information, make sure to ask about the wonderful (and little-known) above-ground hiking trails. The Mammoth Cave National Park is open every day but Christmas. Call (502) 758–2251 or 758–2328 for information.

To date, the navigable cave system in this area is more than 300 miles long. Ask about some of the odd projects the cave provoked, like an underground hospital for tuberculosis victims. The cool, clean cave air would have been good for any victim of lung disease, but smoke from the cooking fires accumulated in the chamber where they lived and killed them quickly. What the doctors needed was more basic than holistic thinking—they needed common sense. Other cave project artifacts include leaching vats that remain from the time when saltpeter (sodium nitrate or potassium nitrate) was extracted for making gunpowder during the War of 1812. Also make sure you hear the whole story of the explorer, Floyd Collins. For many years his casket was on display in the Crystal Onyx Cave, to which he had been searching for a new entrance when he died. In 1929 when local cave owners were competing fiercely for tourists, someone stole Collins's body and dumped it in the Green River because it was a popular attraction. Recently his remains have been reinterred in a less public place.

The American Cave and Karst Center on Main Street in Horse Cave is a brand-new environmental education museum developed by the American Cave Conservation Association, Inc. Their worthy mission is to educate people, especially those who live on karstlands, about how the land works and about how our actions affect the health of the system. Venial sins like dumping trash in sinkholes become mortal sins in karst areas where the whole groundwater system can easily be contaminated. The entrance to Hidden River Cave is accessible through the museum for the first time since 1943. Previously, no one wanted to go near the cave and its underground stream because it reeked of raw sewage.

Other exhibits in the museum include a wall display devoted to bats, a large mural of a cross-section of a karst region, and stories and artifacts from mines, bootlegging operations, early tourist endeavors, prehistoric shelters, and ceremonial sites. For more information, contact: ACCA, Main and Cave Street, P.O. Box 409,

Horse Cave, KY 42749, or call (502) 786–1466. Memorial Day through Labor Day, museum hours are 9:00 A.M. to 5:00 P.M., Monday through Friday, and 1:00 to 5:00 P.M. on weekends.

The Horse Cave Theatre is one of only eight professional theaters in rural America. From late June through early November the company performs five productions per season. The range of genres is broad—Shakespeare, modern comedies, thrillers, and experimental theater by regional playwrights—and thereby maintains a loyal local audience in addition to tourists. Performances run every evening except Monday at the large open-thrust stage in downtown Horse Cave at 107–109 East Main Street. Weekend days also have matinees. Call (502) 786–2177 for information on the current season.

The official Kentucky State Championship Old-Time Fiddling Contest is no place for beginners. Kentucky has some of the hottest fiddlers in the world, and these cream-of-the-crop players are fantastic. This is the only place to have a breakdown; your choice of Tennessee Breakdown, North Carolina Breakdown, Straw Breakdown, or Cheatum County Breakdown. A few fiddlers agreed to put together a little contest to raise money for the March of Dimes, and BOOM—the thing took off. Now the contest is held annually at Rough River Dam State Resort Park in the northern part of Grayson County during the third weekend in July. Call (502) 257–2311 for more information.

East of Bowling Green, the next sizable town is Glasgow, host of the Highland Games and Gathering of Scottish Clans, held near the end of May or in early June at Barren River State Resort Park east of Glasgow on Highway 31. The Games begin with a musical extravaganza called the Tattoo; after that Clan and society members get together, and there's a Tartan Ball and Scottish Country Dancing. Last but not least exciting are the athletic and battleax competitions that originated as martial exercises under King Malcolm Canmore in Scotland around 1060. The best-known aspect of the gathering, however, is the Ceilidh, another set of musical performances by American and international musicians—praised by Fiona Ritchie of National Public Radio's "Thistle and Shamrock" show. For more information, contact The Glasgow Highland Games, Inc., P.O. Box 373, Glasgow, KY 42142, or call (502) 651–3141.

The Hall Place Bed and Breakfast is a handsome place to spend the night and to have a big country ham breakfast. From downtown Glasgow, take Highway 31E south (South Green Street) for 1½ blocks and look for the sign on the right. Although the house was built in 1852, the three B&B rooms have modern private baths, phones, and televisions. Room rates begin at $40.

From Eighty Eight (yes, that's the town's name), take Highways 839 or 163 to the south, to Tompkinsville, the Monroe County seat. Follow Highway 1446 south of town for about 3 miles to the Old Mulkey Meeting House State Shrine. Built in 1804 it is the oldest log meeting house in the state and probably the only example of symbolic log architecture. The building's twelve corners represent the twelve Apostles, and the three doors are meant to be reminders of the Trinity. Daniel Boone's oldest sister, Hannah, is buried in the cemetery alongside other early settlers.

Unassuming as it looks, Tompkinsville has a bizarre reputation to uphold. In early September this town hosts the most popular event in the Monroe County Watermelon Festival, the Privy Grand Prix—yes, an outhouse race. It's professional. The outhouses (3' x 3' x 6' from the ground) must be made of wood (except for the wheels and roofs), and teams must consist of two people pulling, two pushing, and one on the john who must wear a seatbelt, a crash helmet, and weigh at least one hundred pounds. Contestants dream of breaking the toilet paper ribbon in a shower of glory. Of course, the festival's main theme is watermelons, so there has to be a seed-spitting contest. In 1982, the first year of the Privy Grand Prix, the announcer for the spitting contest got tongue-tied and made a first call for "speed-sitting." Thus, serendipity gave birth to a new, perfect name for the outhouse race.

Living History Country

"The pause that refreshes will make husband more helpful." Wives everywhere want to know what kind of pause? At what price? Every experienced consumer knows that it's Coca-Cola, of course, at the cost of five cents per pause in 1934 when the phrase was printed on a drink tray. **Schmidt's Coca-Cola Museum** in the Coca-Cola Bottling Company of Elizabethtown is an I-remember-that-one experience with a dark twist. Go north of town on Highway 31W. In the museum you'll find yourself growing curiously thirsty. These Coca-Cola memorabilia are antiques, but it seems that subliminal (and overt) messages were being employed by advertisers from the beginning. The color red is pervasive and the "Coca-Cola Girls" smile out from every wall, eternally in full bloom. In the beverage's early days it was advertised as a virtual panacea. One poster reads: "The slightly tonic effect of Coca-Cola relieves fatigue and calms overwrought nerves without undue stimulation. It is genuinely good to the taste and aids digestion." Though it is never mentioned in the museum, keep in mind that Coke originally contained a small quantity of cocaine. Now we have only sugar (or Nutra-Sweet) and an almost patriotic penchant for the stuff. Come see one of America's favorite seducers. Hours are Monday through Friday from 9:00 A.M. to 4:00 P.M. There is a small admission fee.

Polarities can be wonderful teachers. Leave the Coke Museum and please please please take time to get an education at the **Emma Reno Connor Black History Gallery.** Go southeast of the courthouse on East Dixie Avenue, veer left onto Hawkins Drive and look immediately for a white stucco house on the right with a sign that says BLACK HISTORY GALLERY painted on a set of black concrete steps in the front yard. This was the childhood home of the late Emma Reno Connor, a teacher who recognized a disgraceful dearth of information about the lives and accomplishments of black people in America. She amended her lesson plans with pictures, articles, and stories of African-Americans and later organized these teaching materials into museum displays.

An amateur museum comprised of well-organized cutouts from magazines, original pen-and-ink portraits of great people, poems by Ms. Connor, and newspaper articles, this is also a powerful place full of love, knowledge, and opportunities to see our culture from another true angle. You'll learn about the lives and accomplishments of Satchmo, Josephine Baker, Langston Hughes, Sojourner Truth, Gwendolyn Brooks, Frederick Douglass, and Martin Luther King, Jr., to name a few outstanding people. Hours are noon to 5:00 P.M., Saturday and Sunday, or as posted. On weekdays, make an appointment with Charles Connor, Emma's widower (502–769–5204) or with her sister Ruby Williams (502–765–7653). A tour of the gallery with Mr. Connor brings nationally known figures to life, Mrs. Williams will tell you the personal histories of local heroes. Together they could change your life.

Many towns of historic significance offer walking tours of the downtowns, but few resurrect the characters in living color. In the summer Elizabethtown gives guided walking tours during which you meet and see a brief "performance" by Sarah Bush Johnston Lincoln (Abe's stepmother), P. T. Barnum, Jenny Lind, Carrie Nation, and eight other characters portrayed by local people dressed in period costumes and well versed in their figure's history. Carrie Nation, for example, runs down the street with a Bible in one hand and her famous hatchet in the other to shut down Jim Neighbor's bar. In real life she was prevented from destroying the place when someone knocked her out with a bar stool. The tour covers twenty-five buildings and requires about an hour. Tours are scheduled for Thursday nights at 7:00 P.M. and start at the Elizabethtown Visitors and Information Commission, 24 Public Square. You can also call (502) 765–2175.

The Olde Bethlehem Academy Inn at 7051 Saint John Road is one of the classiest country inns in the South. The main part of the building was built around 1818 for former governor John Helm; later, it was a Catholic girls' school. In 1989 Mike Dooley bought the place and turned every square foot of the space into functional aspects of his inn. In addition to several conference rooms, there are eight overnight rooms, including suites. A fantastic ballroom on the second floor is in an old chapel with a dome ceiling, brass chandeliers, and a 9-foot mural of Moses with diamonds in each of his eyes (not a comfortable image under which to slow dance). The inn also has a full restaurant, open for lunch on Tuesday through Saturday, 11:00 A.M. to 2:30 P.M.; dinner on Wednesday through Saturday, 5:00 to 9:00 P.M.; and a Sunday buffet from noon to 4:00 P.M. Call (502) 862–9003 for information or reservations.

Another great place for lunch or dinner is south of Elizabethtown in a little railroad community called Glendale. Go south of town on Highway 31W for about 5 miles, and take Highway 222 west to Glendale. In the early 1970s James and Idell Sego transformed the old Glendale hardware store, which is smack-dab next to the railroad tracks on Main Street, into **The Whistle Stop Restaurant** (502–369–8586), where they now serve really really good southern food for reasonable prices in a cozy depotlike atmosphere. Famous for their open-faced hot brown sandwich, a mountain of roast beef on bread smothered with a rich cheese sauce, the restaurant's menu ranges from homemade soups to ham and asparagus rolls to fried chicken and taco salad. Desserts clarify the meaning of sin. Hours are 11:00 A.M. to 9:00 P.M., Tuesday through Saturday.

All of Glendale seems to be in a time warp. Though the village is small, it has a functional general store and several antique and gift shops. During the first weekend in December, every building is decked out for a Christmas in the Country event, open to the public. In the midst of this pretend atmosphere is an 1870s farmhouse with a big inviting front porch. This is the Petticoat Junction Bed & Breakfast at 223 High Street. Five overnight rooms are available, two of which have private baths (one bath has an old-time claw-foot tub, and the other is a state-of-the-art Jacuzzi). Walk-ins are welcome, or you can call (502) 369–8604.

Not everything in the area is caught in the past. Leslie H. Wilmoth and John and Lisa Brittain of the **Nolin River Nut Tree Nursery** have become famous for performing nutty modern-day miracles. Of the more than one hundred varieties of nut trees grown in their nursery, most are grafted. You're not supposed to be able to graft most nut trees because the sap tends to run so much that the grafts don't take (heal and fuse to the rooted tree). These growers make expert use of an obscure method called a coin purse graft. They also are able to dig and ship nut trees up to 5 feet tall—that's 4 feet taller than the "rules" claim is possible without fatally damaging the tap root.

Leslie, John, and Lisa can probably answer any question you have about nut trees and sell you just about any variety your heart desires. For between $14 and $18 per tree, you can choose from a number of walnuts, heartnuts, butternuts, chestnuts, hickories, pecans, hicans (a cross between hickory and pecan), and persimmons. Order as far in advance of spring as possible, and call if you plan to visit. For a catalog, write: Nolin River Nut Tree Nursery, 797 Port Wooden Road, Upton, KY 42784, or call (502) 369–8551.

Abraham Lincoln has put **Hodgenville** on the map and kept it there. From Elizabethtown, take Highway 61 south to Hodgenville and follow signs to the Abraham Lincoln Birthplace National Historic Site, south of town. The humble log cabin in which Abe was born on February 12, 1809, is enshrined in a huge stone, columned building prefaced by fifty-six steps that represent the years of Abe's life. The park is open all day, every day. Go through town on Highway 31E to tour Lincoln's boyhood home on Knob Creek Farm, open daily from April through October. There is a replica of the cabin where young Abe's first memories were formed; this was the last place he lived in Kentucky.

Downtown on Lincoln Square near the bronze statue is a small Lincoln Museum (502–358–3163), open Monday through Saturday, 9:00 A.M. to 6:00 P.M., and Sundays from 1:00 to 6:00 P.M. The museum features twelve scenes from Lincoln's life (with wax figures) and a display of memorabilia. Ask about the Lincoln Days Celebration held in town during the second weekend of October. The festival features a few odd events like Lincoln look-alike contests and a very manly rail-splitting tournament. Call for more information at (502) 358–3411.

Lakes and Knobs Region

Going east from Glasgow, the high road leads to Columbia, the low to Burkesville. Take Highway 80 or the Cumberland Parkway to Columbia. Everyone knows that Lindsey Wilson College is in Columbia, but few people know about the Adair County Bell Pepper Festival, winner of the Kentucky Festival Association's "outstanding festival for its size" award. In many ways it's a good old county fair, but there's more. How about a Bed Race or an Ugly Man Contest or tests of real vocational skill, like the Hay Bale Throwing Contest or Nail Driving Contest? They have a darn good square dance on Monday night. The festival is held the week after Labor Day.

Few people know that on April 29, 1872, Jesse James and his gang held up the Bank of Columbia and killed a cashier named R. C. Martin. Nor do most know that Mark Twain's parents, Jane Lampton and John Marshall Clemens, were married in Columbia in 1823. Fewer still realize Maxwell House Coffee was invented by a Burkesville boy named Joel Owsley Cheek. After a brief career as a traveling (by horseback) salesman, Cheek started experimenting in the late 1870s with roasting and mixing blends of coffee that were usually sold to the stores green and unground. The first place to sell the expensive blend was the Maxwell House hotel in Nashville, Tennessee. The rest is history.

Dale Hollow is a large man-made lake that straddles the Kentucky-Tennessee line. From Burkesville, take any road to the south and watch for signs. The area is full of small marinas, motels, and fishing camps. It is said to be one of the cleanest lakes in the state, and since there are numerous inlets and islands, Dale Hollow is a good place to swim. The two states also share Static, a little town with a rowdy reputation. The town sits directly on the border where Highway 127 goes through; Kentucky says Static belongs in Tennessee, and Tennessee says the town is ours. With a town name that means "showing little change," it's no wonder no one claims the place. To make matters worse, legend has it that Static was named after a local farmer's one-eyed bulldog.

To the north is **Lake Cumberland,** one of the largest man-made lakes in the world; its peak surface area is more than 63,000 acres. It is also said to have more walleye, bass, and crappie than any other American lake. Although water-oriented businesses are all around the lake, you may want to stop by the headquarters of the Lake Cumberland State Resort Park off Highway 127 south of Jamestown to get specific information. If you boat around the big, clear lake, you'll find endless little coves to explore, places to swim, fossils over which to ponder, and almost no commercial development to distract you. Call (502) 343–3111 for more information.

A town named Touristville makes a person suspicious, and rightly so. Some Chamber of Commerce type was on the ball that hot summer day in 1929 when the post office was named. For a time Touristville did profit from the flow of vacationers through nearby Mill Springs, which sits very near what is now Lake Cumberland. Dunagan's Grocery & Supply in Mill Springs now serves as post office for both towns. The anachronistic store is something of an attraction for nostalgia- and curiosity-seekers. In 1935 Everette Dunagan's father moved the store to its present site from about a hundred yards across the road, using one mule and a lot of ingenuity. Since then precious little has changed. Dunagan still has a ham he bought in the early 1960s; he had put it in a plastic bag where it grew frightfully moldy, and no one bought it. Originally it weighed 9 pounds; in 1979 it weighed a mere 6 pounds; in 1984 it was down to about 5 pounds. Now it's a feathery tangle of fibers, more mold than meat.

To get to Mill Springs, go to Monticello in Wayne County and follow Highway 90 to Touristville. Turn west on Highway 1275 and you'll see signs for the **Mill Springs Mill,** "largest overshot water wheel in the world." That's a slightly overrated water wheel, but as it turns out, the wheel, which is 40 feet, 10 inches in diameter, is the third largest in the nation and among the top ten in the world. It may be the only of the biggies to still be functioning as a gristmill. The first cereal grinding mill was built around 1817 at this site where thirteen springs gushed out of the hillside. The water wheel also powered a cotton gin, a carting factory, and a wagon production line. After a fire and several remodelings, the Diamond Roller Mills' 40-foot wheel was installed in 1908. Today the mill is open to the public from Memorial Day to Labor Day, 11:00 A.M. to 5:00 P.M. On weekends they grind cornmeal with the old equipment. Call (606) 679–6337 for more information.

The mill is also the site of a tide-turning Civil War battle in January 1862. Confederate General Felix Kirk Zollicoffer set up camp at the Metcalfe House near the mill. Zollicoffer lost The Battle of Logan's Crossroads and thereby left the first gap in what was a long, strong Rebel defense line in Kentucky. West of Somerset on Highway 80 in a town called Nancy are The Mill Springs National Cemetery and the Zollicoffer burial site, where more than one hundred Confederate troops from the Mill Springs battle are buried under one stone. From the cemeteries you can see (and smell and taste and climb) the fruit trees at the adjacent Haney's Appledale Orchard (606–636–6148), one of the state's best and largest apple orchards. In autumn parts of the orchard are open for U-Pick, and the orchard store sells apples and cider.

If you leave Jamestown and Russell Springs to the north, you leave the lake area and enter the "knobs" again. Take Highway 127 north into Casey County, known as the "Gate Capitol of the World." Most gates, truck racks, and round-bale feeders are made of tubular steel, a concept first developed in 1965 by Tarter Gate in Dunnville, the first and largest of the gate companies in the county, producing over 1,000 gates a day.

Due to the isolation and beauty of this hilly country, a large number of Amish have moved into the area. It's always inspirational to see their neat, well-loved farms, but, of course, they're not interested in intrusion from the outside world. This community has two businesses that are open to the public. Going north on 127 from Russell Springs, turn southeast on Highway 910. Go about 3½ miles and turn east onto South Fork. This beautiful drive takes you past both secular and Amish farms (watch for "shocked" corn and draft horses in the field). It's hilarious to see the contrast in styles: Watch the right side of South Fork for the gaudiest house in the world; the yard is thick with whirligigs, holiday yard art, and endless junk.

Enjoy the Amish way a few miles down at **Bluegrass Wood and Leather Craft:** Furniture, Chairs, Tables, Harnesses and Leather Goods; this remarkable place is run by remarkable people. The store is a large building on the right filled with furniture (mainly in oak) upstairs and leather goods downstairs, all of excellent quality. Due to the fact that the Amish in the area do much of their farming with horses and mules, the leather items are primarily horse-related, but there aren't many limits to this craftsman's ability. The fellows in the shop are more than willing to answer questions, and if you're serious about a purchase, they are glad to take a special order as long as it falls within their way of working. There's no phone, but they are usually open on weekdays during business hours.

Back on Highway 910, go "just a little piece" farther south to Dutchman's Store, a small Amish general store in the basement of their community elementary school. To remain apart as much as possible from the corrupt aspects of our culture, the Amish often employ low-technology methods for farming, building, and living in general. So, if you are in search of something unusual, a modern instance of an old model of any kind of equipment, like a hand pump for your cistern, inquire about it at Dutchman's. Let me also recommend the local sorghum. Alan Oberholtzer, the local molasses meister, keeps this store well stocked. You'll want to speed home wildly to make a mess of biscuits just to have an excuse for draining what promises to be the first of many jars.

To appreciate a style of fine leather craftsmanship that is radically different from the Amish, pay a visit to a tailor of leather motorcycle suits in the northwest corner of Casey County. Lou and Janet Snedden run a bang-up mail-order business called **Lou's Leathers** based way way way out in the boondocks. Their phone number is in one town, their street address in another, and their mailing address is in another county. When I asked Janet for directions, she replied cryptically "Actually, we're not anywhere." The Sneddens love racing motorcycles. They repair and custom-make racing suits for motorcyle, snowmobile, and car racers all over North America and, as of this year, Puerto Rico. Racers usually give the Sneddens an idea of what they want, leaving the specific design and masterful execution to the makers.

If you want to see the Sneddens's craftsmanship in action and don't mind a drive, head north on Highway 127 into Liberty and turn north onto Highway 49. Turn to the west on 1547 and go about 1 mile. When the road splits three ways, take the middle road, Highway 1742, for 4 miles to a four-way intersection and turn right. Take the second gravel road on the right. Lou's Leathers is the first place on the right in a metal building with red trim. Hours are Monday through Thursday, 7:30 A.M. to 5:00 P.M., and Friday until 11:30 A.M. If you get lost, call (606) 787–5029 or 787–6176.

Head south again on Highway 127 and make your way toward Somerset. Along the way, if you want to stop for lunch or dinner, try the general store in the tiny town of Yosemite (pronounced YO-seh-mite). The homemade chili is hot—a liquid atomic fireball. These grocers also make their own pickled eggs. They keep the homemade eggs next to a jar of commercial eggs that are dyed a sickening hot pink. The manager told me it increases sales of the homemade ones. Smart. Yosemite is on Highway 70 going southeast from Liberty. You can stay on Highway 70, which becomes Highway 635 and runs into Highway 27, which leads into Somerset.

Burnside, south of Somerset on Highway 27, is the only town on Lake Cumberland as well as the only town under the lake. In the late 1940s the U.S. Army Corps of Engineers moved the entire town to higher ground as the lake area was being impounded. The durable remains of old Burnside become visible during the winter when the lake's level is lowered. It's eerie seeing foundations, porch steps, and sidewalks, emerge from the mud and debris. Nearby is General Burnside State Park, a 400-acre island surrounded by Lake Cumberland and used for camping, fishing, boating, and all the usual lakeside fooling-around.

If you aren't camping and need lodging, Somerset has one bed and breakfast. The Shadwick House at 411 South Main Street has been a guest house for more than seventy years and has remained in family hands. The present owners are the great-grandchildren of Nellie Stringer Shadwick, who built the place in 1920. Six rooms are available at the nightly rate of $25 for a double and $21 for a single, including breakfast.

Stab, a short name for a small town with a short creek, is 10 miles east of Somerset on Highway 80 near the Pleasant Run Baptist Church. Short Creek emerges from a hillside cavern at an impressive width of about 25 feet. It flows in a semicircle for maybe 150 feet and ducks back underground into a small cave. There's no doubt, this is the shortest creek in the world. Elwood

Taylor, who owns the creek, says that there used to be a gristmill at one end and that the creek was often used for wintertime baptisms because the water is always 54 degrees Fahrenheit. The Taylors own the small grocery at Stab. Stop by their store and ask permission to have a picnic by the creek. You may hear some good stories.

Cumberland Falls is not really off the beaten path, but it's such a flamboyant, unusual cataract that it must be recognized. Follow Interstate 75 to Corbin, get off on Highway 25W, veer west on Highway 90, and follow the signs to Cumberland Falls State Resort Park (606–528–4121). The wide, humble Cumberland River explodes dramatically as it crashes over the curving precipice and becomes the largest American waterfalls east of the Rocky Mountains, except, of course, for Niagara. When the entire disk of the moon is illuminated and the skies are clear, a long moonbow arches from the top of the falls to the turbulent waters below. The only other moonbow in the world is at the Victoria Falls in Africa. The Cumberland Falls are so powerful that the mist fans way out and above the water, and when the wind is right, you get a gentle shower on the rocks at the top. More than 65 feet high and 125 feet across, the falls are believed to have retreated as far as 45 miles upstream from their original position near Burnside. This was accomplished over tens of thousands of years as the water wore away the soft sandstone under the erosion-resistant lip at the top.

The park, which is open all year, has another smaller but beautiful falls called Eagle Falls. If it's hot, the pool below Eagle Falls is a divine swimming hole. Ask for information at the park lodge about hiking trails, rooms, cabins, and special events. Within the park is a nature preserve left to its wild state. It boasts more than fifteen species of rare plants and animals, including federally endangered mussels and rare plants like the box huckleberry, brook saxifrage, goat's rue, and riverweed. A guided hike can be a real education.

Another way to "get into" the river and to have a rip-roaring good time is to hook up with a guided canoeing or whitewater rafting trip down the river. Write: Sheltowee Trace Outfitters, P.O. Box 1060, Whitley City, KY 42653, or call (800) 541–RAFT.

The other big playground in this region is at the Big South Fork National River and Recreation Area in McCreary County, Kentucky, and below the border. Take Highway 27 or Interstate 75 south to Highway 92 and go west to Stearns. If you're arriving via

Highway 27, check out the natural rock bridge off Highway 927, which goes to Nevelsville. You can also get to Big South Fork on Highway 700, which intersects Highway 27 near Whitley City. The latter route brings you directly to Yahoo Falls, gorgeous cataracts that, although small in volume, are the highest falls in the state.

The whole Big South Fork area is beautiful. Deep jagged gorges are frequent surprises and the variations in the landscape, from cool woods to hot, high, open-faced rocks, are endlessly pleasing. That the area was once extensively logged and mined is apparent. From early April through the end of October the Forest Service operates a scenic railway that takes visitors into an abandoned coal mining camp called **Blue Heron,** or Mine 18. The remnants of the isolated community are eerie and bring to life some of what you may know about company towns. The Stearns Museum (606–376–5730) fills out the picture with historic artifacts. The sandstone tree stump in front of the museum was recently unearthed in a strip mine just below the Tennessee line. Apparently the two-ton stump is not petrified wood but is a sandstone cast of a tree (possibly an oak) that died about 315 million years ago. When the tree rotted or dissolved, the space was filled with sandstone silt that hardened.

On the south side of Williamsburg at the intersection of Interstate 75 with Highway 92 is **Bailey's Country Store,** perhaps the only general store/radio station in the state. Bart, Ed, Bob, and Joe Bailey run the store and the station, WCCT in Corbin, with a little money and a lot of humor. The boys' father, Virgil, opened the store in 1939 and started the live radio show in 1947 mainly for advertising purposes. The show is hilarious as is the "studio," a control board on a plastic laminate-topped dinette by a store window overlooking a cow pasture. All the brothers are funny; they give advice, advertise goods for sale, announce funerals and lost dogs, and make general observations about life. The show is broadcast live every day but weekends and Wednesdays. If you need a mule or a set of boxsprings, give a listen.

Jellico, Tennessee, across the border on Interstate 75 is (or was) the number one place for underage Kentuckians to get hitched. In Jellico they do it fast, legal, and without parental or priestly consent. "I do and he does too."

East of Williamsburg is **Mulberry Friendship Center,** one of many fruitful mountain craft cooperatives in the Appalachian region. Because this one is near a beaten path, the folks are prepared to show visitors around. The women who quilt here regularly often have some beauties for sale at the center. Activities change, so call ahead at (606) 549–1617. From Williamsburg, go 9 miles east on Highway 92, turn right (southeast) on Highway 904, and watch for the sign.

Corbin sits on the adjoining corners of Whitley, Laurel, and Knox counties and serves as the commercial hub for the whole area. Although Corbin is not famous worldwide, its native son Colonel Harland Sanders is. From Tokyo to Moscow to London, England, and London, Kentucky, the Colonel's red-and-white portrait, complete with his almost-sinister goatee, smiles at chicken consumers everywhere from his Kentucky Fried Chicken franchises. Corbin is the home of the original restaurant—it's even listed on the National Register of Historic Places! At **The Harland Sanders Café & Museum,** see Harland's kitchen as it was in the 1940s and eat in a dining area restored to resemble the original restaurant. Go north of Corbin and take Highway 25E south; turn right at the second traffic light.

Another oldie found in few places farther north than Corbin is SONIC, the notorious, junky, 1950s-style, fast-food drive-in with a yellow roof and speakers on poles in each parking space. Times were when you could fulfill your craving for a famous Sonic Burger anywhere. Get it while you can in Corbin on the east side of Highway 25E.

London, the next town to the north, is trying to get in on the chicken action, too; it has started an annual World Chicken Festival held downtown at the end of September. In addition to the usual festival activites, all the great cooks in town compete for coveted cook-off prizes. The winners, of course, are the tasters. Call (606) 878–6900 for information.

If you think the interstate near London looks busy now in a post-industrial, highway-laced world, ponder the years between 1775 and 1800 when more than 300,000 people came into Kentucky from the east through this area when it was wild. **The Levi Jackson State Park** is situated at the intersection of the Wilderness Road and Boone's Trace, the two main frontier "highways." The park is 2 miles south of London on Highway 25. The Mountain Life Museum gives newcomers to the area a glimpse of pioneer history with a reproduction pioneer settlement stocked with period furniture and Indian artifacts. Also at the park is McHargue's Mill, a completely restored, operational gristmill, circa 1812, that serves as a kind of mill museum and has what may be the world's largest collection of millstones. On the park grounds is the only marked burial ground along the Wilderness Road (though historians believe that there are many other cemeteries lacking headstones). Ask about hiking and camping in the park. For any park information, call (606) 878–8000.

A visit to **Minnie's Gourd-Craft Museum** will be among the best-spent hours in your life. Get off Interstate 75 in London and take Highway 25 north to Highway 490; go a short distance and turn onto Highway 30. Minnie Black's place is a stone house at the road's intersection with Highway 3434. Open by appointment only, call (606) 843–7447 as far in advance as possible. If you can see Minnie Black wearing a bright red hat made of dried loofah gourds and feathers, strumming her turtle-back banjo, and singing a zippy tune, you'll find it hard to believe she was born in 1898. You'll also be shocked at the immaculate condition of her gardens and the wild, whimsical character of her work. Her self-appointed task in late life is to grow gourds and to create as many zany pieces of sculpture from the inedible fruits as her imagination supplies.

Minnie likes to have fun. After her husband died, she began going to the Senior Citizens Center in London. There she organized a band and supplied the musicians with gourd instruments. Gourds taller than she are equipped with strings and tuning pegs to make a bass; harmonicas mounted in the side of a bright blue whale gourd make the players look more than ridiculous; various prehistoric or fantastic animals filled with seeds and stones become percussive shakers; and wild curling gourds, usually three-headed beasts, form kazoo holders. Minnie's Gourd Band was a national hit. She was featured on "P.M. Magazine," "Good Morning America," "The David Letterman Show," and "The Tonight Show."

The little museum building in front of the house is filled with gourd creatures—monkeys on strings, gourd-asaurs, weird lizards and snakes, cave men, satirical political figures, a 4-foot Statue of Liberty, a 3-foot tall elephant, anteaters, porcupines, and so on. All this is born of a gardenful of gourds, some self-hardening sculpture medium, paint, and the wacky imagination of a young-old woman. Though the band has dissolved, Minnie Black is still sculpting and still laughing. For your spiritual health, meet her and be inspired.

The next town to the north is Mt. Vernon. Mt. Vernon is considered a kind of gateway to the Knobs, the serious hills that skirt the Appalachian mountains. For a double delight—beautiful mountains and wonderful people—take a drive straight uphill from the caution light in downtown Mt. Vernon at the junction of Highways 150 and 1249. Exactly 10 miles later you'll find yourself on a hillside in front of Betty Thomas's red-brick ranch house on the left. She works at home and welcomes visitors but requests that you call first at (606) 256–5378 to see her fine dolls and stuffed animals. She makes realistic Canada geese and goslings, decoy-sized mallard ducks, debonair foxes dressed in traditional hunt clothing and hard hats, old-world-style teddy bears, mice, cats, dogs, unicorns, soft-sculptured baby dolls, and many others. Most of her pieces have hinged joints, and all are stuffed so tightly that they stand independently; all are made of high-quality wool, satin, or cotton in delicious colors.

Ms. Thomas's patience, persistence, and skill with her hands come by her honestly. Her parents raised thirteen children in a log cabin in a holler across the road from her present home. Her father, William McClure, is rightfully considered a kind of legend among folk culture enthusiasts. For years his handmade wooden roof shingles were in constant demand in all of the surrounding states, as were his handsome carved dough bowls. You can see some of his work on the roof of the Aunt Polly Hiatt house at Renfro Valley. They say that although that roof has gaps in it so big you can see sky through them, it doesn't leak a drop. Long live the McClure family!

Here's the line-up: "Banjo Pickin' Gal," "Winking at Me," "Chicken Reel," "Cackling Hen," "Barbara Allen," "Poor Ellen Smith," "Tramp on the Street," "Matthew 24," and "Old Shep." These could be the names of thoroughbreds in the starting gate at the Derby but are, in fact, some of the best country songs ever written and some of the first ever performed at **Renfro Valley,** "Kentucky's Country Music Capital." Many folks in the region remember when they first heard John Lair's silk-smooth voice in 1939, broadcasting an all-country-music radio show live from his big tobacco barn in Rockcastle County. Those humble beginnings have led to the establishment of a large complex of buildings and year-round traditional music and entertainment programs at Renfro Valley; the radio shows are now transmitted to more than 200 stations in North America. In addition to performance events in the auditorium (a luxury barn), there are on the grounds a craft village with mountain craft demonstrators, a gift shop, the Renfro Valley Museum, a bakery, a hotel, and a restaurant. Go north from Mt. Vernon a few miles on Highway 25, for the more scenic route, to the Renfro Valley exit. Call for more information, show tickets, or reservations at (800) 765–7464.

Off the Beaten Path in Western Kentucky

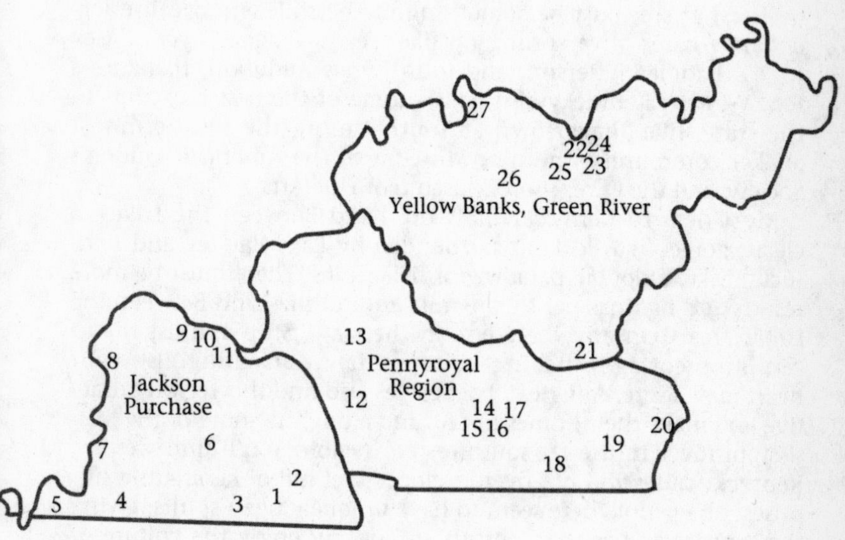

1. National Museum of the Boy Scouts of America
2. House of Willow
3. Bell City Pottery
4. Henson Broom Shop
5. Reelfoot Lake
6. Wooldridge Monuments
7. Columbus-Belmont Battle-field State Park
8. Wickliffe Mounds Research Center
9. Metropolis Lake State Nature Preserve
10. *Wacinton*
11. Museum of the American Quilter's Society
12. Land Between the Lakes
13. Adsmore
14. Pennyroyal Area Museum
15. Trail of Tears Intertribal Indian Pow Wow
16. J. B. Crockett's Lone Oak Restaurant
17. Pete's Custom Saddle Shop
18. Penchem Tack Store
19. The Dutch House
20. Shakertown at South Union
21. Lake Malone Inn
22. Sassafras Tree
23. Owensboro Area Museum
24. Owensboro Museum of Fine Art
25. Mount Saint Joseph Center
26. Diamond Lake Catfish Farm
27. John James Audubon State Park

Western Kentucky

The sky seems bigger in the vast, open land of this western region. Sunsets are beautiful, and you can see a storm coming for hours. There's plenty of room for everyone, and everyone's here—from coal miners and bluegrass musicians to Amish farmers and master quilters. There must be something in the soil here because legendary figures have sprung up like weeds—Edgar Cayce, Casey Jones, Thomas Jefferson, and John James Audubon, to name a few. Western Kentucky also boasts some of the best museums in the state, like Shakertown at South Union, the southernmost Shaker community, the new Museum of the American Quilter's Society, and the Owensboro Museum of Fine Art.

Most dear to Kentuckians is the Land Between the Lakes, a clean, gorgeous wild land surrounded by Lake Barkley and Kentucky Lake, a double paradise for fisherfolks. There must be more resorts and marinas per square mile around the Land Between the Lakes area than anywhere else in the state. Stop and ask about camping, cottages, fishing, restaurants, or anything else your heart may desire. American bald eagles also find this region attractive and make their homes in LBL and along the shore of the Mississippi River in the far southwestern region. You'll find western Kentucky quiet and not overdeveloped, yet full of fascinating surprises. The people here seem to have uniquely open spirits, giving the traveler a chance to absorb and deeply enjoy the culture of this place.

Jackson Purchase

On the fourth Sunday in May, if you are anywhere near Benton, west of the lakes on Highway 641, plan to attend "Big Singing Day," the only American singing festival that uses the 1835 Southern Harmony Book of shape note tunes. This wonderfully nonhierarchical group singing event has been happening here since 1843. There is no leader and no instrumental accompaniment, and the songs, usually traditional Welsh hymns, are arranged in parts such that no one sings beyond their range. The other big event is Benton's Tater Day, held on the first Monday in April since 1843, the world's only event dedicated to the sweet potato. Pay homage to a great food and enjoy a friendly small-town festival.

Going south on Highway 641 brings you to the peaceful town of Murray, which Rand McNally ranked "number one retirement location in the country" because of the proximity of outdoor recreational areas, the low crime rate, and the low cost of living. On the Murray State University campus you can get a free crash course in the history of the region by visiting the Wrather West Kentucky Museum. Hours are Monday through Friday from 10:00 A.M. to 5:00 P.M., and Saturday from 10:00 A.M. to 2:00 P.M. The Clara M. Eagle Gallery on the fourth floor of the Doyle Fine Arts Building on the corner of Olive and Fourteenth streets features a wide variety of exhibits, from faculty shows to nationally touring exhibitions of fine art and craft. For gallery information, call (502) 762–3052.

One of Murray's best-known attractions is the **National Museum of the Boy Scouts of America** at the corner of Calloway Avenue and Sixteenth Street. For Scouts, the best part will be the Gateway Park, an outdoor ropes and teams course (like the COPE courses). Boy Scouts, Cub Scouts, or any other group with members at least eleven years old can take courses during the day by reservation. The museum owns fifty-three original Norman Rockwell paintings. In 1912 when Rockwell was only eighteen years old, he was hired as an illustrator by *Boys' Life* magazine. From 1912 to 1976 he painted hundreds of idealistic, humorous, all-American Scout scenes. For kids, the indoor museum includes high-tech, robot-guided exhibits, low-tech storytelling, decision-making games, and simulated adventure courses. The museum is open June 1 through Labor Day, 9:00 A.M. to 5:00 P.M. Admission is $3 to $6, according to age and activities. Call (502) 762–3383.

For lodging in Murray, consider The Diuguid House Bed and Breakfast at 603 Main Street (502–753–5470). Helena and Lorene Celano bake fresh muffins or fritters as early as you care to rise, and the Victorian house affords you all kinds of spaces for living, from private nooks for reading to a large veranda for socializing.

Speaking of socializing, Rudy's Restaurant on the east side of the courthouse square is so crowded at lunchtime that you may have to sit with a stranger if you're determined to have one of their fresh hamburgers and homemade onion rings. This little place has been open since the early 1930s when the original Rudy made it famous for its consistently good country cooking and cutting-edge gossip. Rudy, a short, roly-poly fellow whose lip never knew the absence of a cigar, collected money and spread the news of the day from a stool behind the big brass cash register. Monday through Friday, breakfast starts at 6:00 A.M., and lunch ends at 2:00 P.M.

Take Highway 94 East and go about 4 miles out of downtown Murray. Look for a small log cabin on the left side of the road with chairs in the yard and a sign by the driveway that reads **House of Willow.** George Beard is an extraordinary, thrifty chairmaker. Regardless of the fact that this style of outdoor furniture, sometimes called "stick furniture," is in vogue at the moment, Mr. Beard's craft has lasting integrity. Like the gypsies who sold his mother willow chairs in the early 1930s, George and his family go to the riverbanks to gather red and white willow limbs that are then bent and nailed into place while still green. Nothing is wasted; the large stock is used for heavy supports, and the thin branches are twisted into decorative backs or armrests. Sit in any chair, love seat, or rocker, and your body will understand that the Shakers couldn't have designed them better. His choices of branch size and spacing create a simple and visually stunning effect. Today George Beard has become something of a regional treasure. In 1978 the Smithsonian Institute bought one of his hooded chairs in red willow for their permanant collection; a dark red Indian willow love seat is in a museum in Utah; and the Kentucky Musuem in Frankfort exhibits a settee and a child's chair. This is a craftsperson not to miss. You can call him at (502) 753–9545.

To find a pottery, look for a chimney. From Murray, take Highway 94 west to Tri City, turn south on Highway 97, and look for the **Bell City Pottery.** Stacks from huge, sixty-year-old, gas-fired kilns rise high behind a rambling cement-block building on the left side of the road. The James Nance family has owned and operated this pottery for about seventy years. In the past, most of the pieces were wheel-thrown, or "turned" as they say in Bell City, but now production is geared toward slip-casting yard art like pink spraypainted "mingoes" (the local term for yard flamingoes), hoboes, and baby deer. Down the road another ½-mile is the distribution center for the pottery, a small retail sales area, and a concrete casting business run by Tommy Nance, nephew of James Nance II, the owner. With a few simple tools, Tommy makes hundreds of concrete birdbaths and outdoor planters each year. Both the clay and the concrete businesses are somewhat modernized versions of America's oldest craft industry. Getting a detailed look at the daily-life realities of a production clayworks is worth your while. Bell City Pottery is a larger but less-known version of Bybee Pottery (near Richmond) and, because of its isolation, the craftspeople are also less dulled by tourism. They close during very cold weather.

As you leave Bell City, going north on Highway 97, watch for Murdocks' Mausoleum, a semi-underground building with a sign on the top that reads, STOP SEE A ROAD MAP TO HEAVEN. Who wouldn't stop? On the wall of the porch is a large painted sign describing how one can get to heaven—the Gospel of John is heavily quoted. Behind a decorative iron door and window, one can view the burial area. The graves of two women take up perhaps a sixth of the burial space, leaving the rest free for future occupants.

The fence-sitting towns of Fulton, Kentucky, and South Fulton, Tennessee, host an annual Banana Festival during the third week in September. That's right, bananas in Kentucky. The festival, which was started in 1962, commemorates the spirit of an era when wholesalers from all over the country came to Fulton to buy bananas that had been shipped from South America to New Orleans and brought by rail to the largest icehouse in the United States, in Fulton. From here the bananas were distributed in the North. In addition to the usual festival activities, the world's largest banana pudding travels the streets of both downtowns on a float during the grand parade and is then served to everyone, free of charge. Normally the pudding weighs one ton, but in order to make the pages of *The Guinness Book of World Records,* a two-ton pudding has been made. Follow Highway 94 west from Murray to Highway 45; go south into town and put on your best yellow tie.

Get back on Highway 94 and go west to Cayce. On the west side of town, look for the **Henson Broom Shop.** A meticulously kept horse barn behind the house is actually Richard N. Henson's broom-making shop. With a few simple pieces of equipment, three generations of skill, piles of sticks, heaps of broom straw, and lots of energy, Henson makes graceful, functional brooms. His grandfather, also Richard N. Henson, started making brooms in 1930 when the American economy was faltering and the family needed more income. Henson's grandfather liked to say, "A Hoover put me into business, and a Hoover put me out of business," referring to the president and the vacuum cleaner, respectively.

Today this third-generation broom-maker is rarely out of work. During the summer and fall Henson converts his horse trailer into a portable workshop, dons a costume, and travels to festivals where he does historic craft reenactment, educating the public while he works. Brooms have changed very little during the last hundred years. One can easily imagine one of his "rustic" brooms leaning by a cooking hearth, but even his heavier utility brooms have strong, traditional shapes. Only his label reveals the objects' modernity. Prices range from $4 to $15. He's glad to have visitors, so stop by anytime. You can call him at (502) 838–6652, or write him at Box 289, (Cayce) Hickman, KY 42050.

R. N. Henson likes his town, and although the mailing address is in Hickman, he puts Cayce on his business cards. Another young man who put this town on the map was the daredevil railroad engineer John Luther Jones (better known as Casey Jones), who was "yanked-up" here. When he got his first job with Illinois Central, there were so many Joneses that his boss nicknamed him "Cayce." The legend that developed around him after his death somehow also corrupted the spelling to "Casey," but folks here haven't forgotten.

In downtown Hickman, next to the Chamber of Commerce at 109A Clinton Street (on the right) is Glass Designs, Sandra Holland's small stained glass studio. She works primarily on commissioned pieces, but a few items are for sale in the store. She also sells stained glass–making supplies, and seeing her work laid out in various stages of completion may cause you to buy some and dash home to start soldering. You can call her at (502) 236–3242.

To the left of the Chamber is the shop of J. M. Cooper, old-world-style tinkerer extraordinaire. Although he makes and repairs guns and jewelry, Cooper is best known for his work on clocks. The shop is filled with all kinds of modern and antique clocks, some of his own, some belonging to townspeople (the mayor told me that J. M. has had at least ten of her clocks for at least a decade), but his pride and joy rises high above everything else on the bluff—the courthouse clock. In 1974 J. M. completely rebuilt the innards of the old Seth Thomas, originally installed in 1904. The clock parts weigh almost two tons, the bell about 2,800 pounds, and the striking hammer a hefty 40 pounds. Few such clocks are in operation, and fewer yet are still wound by hand; every eight days "Coop" climbs the long stairs of the clock tower and winds. On slow days he'll take visitors up with him.

Follow Highway 94 west out of town to **Reelfoot Lake.** The part of the lake that is in Kentucky (most is in Tennessee) is wild, beautiful swampland. During the winter of 1811–12, a series of earthquakes along the New Madrid fault shook the whole region so violently that the tremors made bells ring as far away as Pittsburgh, Pennsylvania. Reelfoot Lake was created when the quakes caused the Mississippi River to run backwards; when it returned to its usual flow, it straightened out and left behind one of its old curves. Look at your map and the abandoned bend will become obvious. Admire the large stands of bald cypress trees. Their lower trunks are broad, flairing like upside-down flying buttresses; the needles are feathery and fine; and they are surrounded by their own "knees," or cone-shaped roots that seem to emerge from the water independently. These roots make it possible for the large trees to remain upright in the muddy soils. Follow Highway 94 southwest to the Reelfoot Lake National Wildlife Refuge and talk to the rangers about the local wildlife.

The only way to go farther west in Kentucky is to drive down Highway 94 into Tennessee where it becomes Highway 78. From Tiptonville, Tennessee, follow the signs to the Madrid Bend, also known as Kentucky Bend or Bessie Bend. A few families have the peninsula to themselves to farm however they please.

In the center of the Jackson Purchase region is the town of Mayfield, known to outsiders for **The Wooldridge Monuments,** "the strange procession that never moves," in the Maplewood Cemetery. The entrance to the cemetery is in town at the intersection of the Highway 45 overpass and North Seventh Street. The eighteen-figure group in sandstone and Italian marble was erected in the late 1890s by an otherwise inconsequential bloke named Henry G. Wooldridge. Though he is the only person buried on the site, the figures represent Wooldridge on his favorite horse, Fop; Wooldridge again standing by a podium; two hounds, a fox and a deer; his three sisters, four brothers, mother, and two great-nieces, one of which, rumor has it, actually resembles Henry's first love, Minnie, who died in her youth. Legend has it that when the statues were en route from Paducah, a drunk climbed on the flat railcar and mounted the stone horse behind the stone Wooldridge and rode into Mayfield, the drunk king of a dumb parade.

A great place to eat in town is the Hills Drive Inn, Since 1949, on West Broadway at the **Y** in the road. They're known for homemade pies and any-way-you-want-it sandwiches. There's a big porch for summer eating, a drive-in window, indoor tables, and a long, sociable counter. The decor has definite allure. I tried, in vain, to buy an old tin John Ruskin cigar sign—BEST AND BIGGEST.

Fiery debates and pit barbecue are at the heart of the Fancy Farm Picnic, perhaps the sole survivor of grass-roots political campaign picnics in America. *The Guinness Book of World Records* lists it as the world's largest one-day picnic, not surprising when more than 15,000 pounds of fresh pork and mutton are cooked annually. The first Saturday in August, beginning at 10:00 A.M., games and entertainment start, country goods booths go up, and local, state, and national political figures rile the crowds, one way or another. Speeches are given from a red, white, and blue bunting-covered flatbed wagon, just like in 1880, when the picnic was established as the last opportunity for candidates to meet before the August primaries. Because the primaries are now held in May, the picnic functions as a debate for the final candidates. Fancy Farm is 10 miles west of Mayfield on Highway 80 at its junction with Highway 339.

Due west on Highway 80 in Hickman County is the low-lying river town of Columbus. Slightly upriver, the **Columbus-Belmont Battlefield State Park** is perched on 200-foot palisades. The park marks the Civil War site of the westernmost Confederate fortification in Kentucky. Rebel soldiers installed a whopping mile-long chain, held afloat by wooden rafts, across the Mississippi River to prevent Union gunboats from moving south. Each link of the chain weighed fifteen pounds, and the anchor attached to it was six tons. Cannon were lined up on the face of the bluffs. Shortly after the fortification was complete, Union forces led by Ulysses S. Grant took the town in 1861 when Confederate forces were crumbling everywhere. It's a pleasantly dizzying picnic and camping site, and the park has a little museum of early Indian artifacts and Civil War relics, like the massive chain links, the anchor, and several cannon from the river blockade.

Hickman County is missing a tooth. At some time between 1820 and 1870, a channel of the Mississippi River shifted to the east, leaving a 9,000-acre chunk of Kentucky land stranded in Missouri, nearly a mile west of the rest of the county. Despite its relocation, in 1871 the Supreme Court awarded the land, now called Wolf Island, to Kentucky, thereby denying the big daddy of all waters the power to move official boundaries.

Follow Highway 123 north to Bardwell, then take Interstate 51 north to Wickliffe. Every Memorial Day weekend from Wickliffe to Fulton, on the Tennessee border, Highway 51 is lined with flea markets and yard sales. If you can't find the junk of your heart's desire on that weekend, you ain't gonna find it.

Go through Wickliffe as if you were crossing the river to Cairo, Illinois, and look for signs to **The Wickliffe Mounds Research Center** (502–335–3681). You'll understand why the Mississippian Indians chose this site as a town or ceremonial grounds when you stand on the highest mound and look out toward the wide, sparkling junction of two massive rivers, the Ohio and the Mississippi. The scene is exhilarating. In addition to the intact four-sided, flat-topped ceremonial mound, three excavation areas have been preserved and interpreted for the public.

Human remains and burial goods are slowly being moved from the Cemetery Building to protected storage areas for further study before a final reinterment for which contemporary Choctaw Indians will perform the appropriate ceremonies. Without being eerie or morbid, the space is moving. The bodies were buried close together, each surrounded by a few significant belongings, each facing east as if to remain in contact with the cycle of days and nights. The display explains how archaeologists determine diet, illnesses, typical injuries, and physical appearances by analyzing the remains of people who weren't radically different from us. Hours are 9:00 A.M. to 4:30 P.M. daily from March to November. Admission is charged. If you want to try your hand at excavation, check into summer field school at the Mounds. Write: Wickliffe Mounds Research Center, P.O. Box 155, Wickliffe, KY 42087.

About 6 miles northeast of Wickliffe on Highway 60 is the town of Barlow, and in it a new museum called the Barlow House Museum, on the corner of Broadway and Fifth Street. The museum pays tribute to the early history of Ballard County by preserving the home and belongings of a family that helped settle the region. The fully restored 1903 Victorian home is open to the public for tours and also for meetings, receptions, and so forth. Contact Tom and Shirley Barlow for more information at (502) 443–7256.

If you've become hooked on digressions, here's an opportunity to indulge. In pursuit of a good story and a scenic drive, continue on Highway 60 east to La Center and take Highway 358 north, then go west on Highway 473 through Ogden (once called Needmore) to Monkey's Eyebrow, no more than a cluster of houses but the most debated place name in the state of Kentucky. There is no post office, hence no official name, but we argue na'theless. Byron Crawford submits the idea that, if one looks at the shape of the northern boundary of Ballard County, the Ohio River forms a rough profile of a monkey in such a way that this community is just where the eyebrow would be. Others say that there was a store owned by John and Dodge Ray, the brothers who settled the sandy loam ridge in the late nineteenth century, and behind the store was a berm that resembled a monkey's eyebrow because it was covered with tall grasses. New theories are welcome fuel for the fire.

Back on Highway 60, go east until you reach Future City. Turn left (northeast) on Highway 996 and go almost 6 miles where the road ends in a strange, swampy landscape at the **Metropolis Lake State Nature Preserve.** The Kentucky State Nature Preserves Commission has purchased Metropolis Lake in order to protect this intriguing little naturally formed body of water and the river floodplain that surrounds it from destructive development. Fishing is permitted here because anglers love the lake's population of fish and because people take good care of the area. Although the lake area was once a developed commercial recreation area, today it is a more pure, enchanted dreamscape with bald cypress and swamp tupelo trees casting strange shapes against the sky and even stranger reflections on the water. Beavers, kingfishers, wildflowers, and seven rare aquatic species are among the many living creatures sharing this special space. If you have questions, call the commission at (502) 564–2886.

Stay on Highway 60 and go east into Paducah, the urban center of the Jackson Purchase region. As you near the downtown area, look for Noble Park on the west side of the road. Stop when you are haunted by an enormous sculpture of a Chickasaw Indian. The piece, called ***Wacinton,*** or "to have understanding," was carved from a 56,000-pound red oak tree by Hungarian-born sculptor Peter "Wolf" Toth in 1985. Toth donated the piece to the city of Paducah and the state of Kentucky in honor of the Native American people who lived in the area before the Jackson Purchase in 1818. At the age of twenty-five, in 1972, Toth decided to carve a giant Indian sculpture for every state in the Union. He refuses pay. His "trail of whispering giants" is a gift to our national conscience. He identifies with the suffering of Native Americans because he and his family lost everything when they fled Hungary in 1956 before the communist revolution. Paducah's *Wacinton* is his fiftieth sculpture. After the United States, he says he'll be carving in Canada, then Mexico.

The people of Paducah have renovated and preserved a once dilapidated Classical Revival–style mansion by making it into the Whitehaven Tourist Welcome Center, south of town on Interstate 24, and filling it with antique furniture from the area. You can get travel information here or call the center at (502) 554–2077. Tours of the mansion are available from 1:00 to 4:00 P.M. daily.

In downtown Paducah between Broadway and Kentucky Avenue is The Market House, the hub of business and trade since 1836. Today the building houses three arts organizations. The Market House Museum (502–443–7759) is a regional history

Wacinton

museum that includes the reconstructed interior of an 1877 drugstore. Hours are noon to 4:00 P.M., Tuesday through Saturday, and 1:00 to 5:00 P.M. on Sunday. The Paducah Art Guild Gallery and gift shop (502–442–2453) has a permanent collection and hangs traveling exhibitions. Hours are noon to 4:00 P.M., Tuesday through Saturday, and 1:00 to 5:00 P.M. on Sunday, except in the summer, when the gallery opens at 10:00 A.M. Also in the building is the Market House Theatre (502–444–6828), a not-for-profit community theater—check their busy production schedule.

Across the street, the Paducah Harbor Plaza is a five-story yellow-brick building with stained glass windows and ornate sandstone cornices. Beverly and David Harris have opened a bed and breakfast on the second floor, making accommodations available in high style as they were when the place was called the Hotel Belvedere. For $40 a night, one or two people get a renovated bedroom, a continental breakfast, and a tour of the McKinley Antique Auto Collection on the first floor. Call (502) 442–2698 for reservations.

You can sleep with the ghost of a heroine at the Farley Place Bed and Breakfast (502–442–2488). Follow Third Street east from downtown and turn left on Clements Street, then right on Farley Place. This big Victorian house was once home to Mrs. Emily Gant Jarrett, a dyed-in-the-wool Rebel who stole the Confederate flag from its pole minutes before General Grant took the city and hid it, perhaps under her dress, while Union soldiers searched her home for it, in vain.

"Short, fat, thin, and tall, Old Skinhead will try to feed you all." I quote from the menu cover at The Skinhead Restaurant, 1020 South Twenty-first Street, the best place for breakfast in Paducah. Owner and prevailing personality Jim Skaggs is totally bald, and he seems to like it because when he opened the place in 1972, he called it by his own nickname, Skinhead. It's as simple as that. The cook arrives at 3:00 A.M. to have homemade biscuits and gravy piping hot by 5:00 A.M. when the doors open. Homestyle plate lunches like fried chicken, chuck wagon, and vegetables are served until 2:00 P.M. Call (502) 442–6471.

When people think of Kentucky crafts, quilts are often the first items that come to mind. As of April 1991, Paducah may also come to mind as the quilt capital of America, thanks to the brand-new **Museum of the American Quilter's Society** (502–898–7903), downtown at the corner of Second and Jefferson streets. Even those of us who have grown up around (or under) handmade quilts and taken them for granted can't help but be awestruck with the beauty of the quilts in endless rows. Unlike many of the quilt collections in the region, this museum is primarily devoted to the modern quilt. Appreciators of abstract painting may find a new passion in the bold shapes and colors of these functional "canvasses."

In addition to the main display area of quilts from the permanant collection and those in traveling exhibitions, the new 30,000-square-foot building has a climate-controlled vault, a bookstore and gift shop, classrooms, and a research library. The organization hosts an enormous annual quilt show and contest the fourth week of April at Paducah's Executive Inn Riverfront, during which 400 quilts from all over the world are displayed and judged for lucrative prizes. If Grandma only knew! Be sure to plan way in advance for the show. The museum is open Tuesday through Saturday, 10:00 A.M. to 5:00 P.M. Admission is $3. For more information, write to the American Quilter's Society, P.O. Box 3290, Paducah, KY 42002.

On a much lighter note and concerning a very different art, Velma Hamock, owner of the Hamock Bowles Funeral Home at 429 South Seventh Street rightfully claims to run the only funeral home in town that's never without a corpse. Yes, it's true. Charles Henry Atkins, known at work as "Speedy" for his fast tobacco stripping, was fishing on the Ohio River in 1928, when he fell in and drowned. Lacking money and relations, he couldn't be buried, so A. Z. Hamock, the funeral director, did some experiments on his body with a homemade embalming fluid. Speedy is still around. The fluid plasticized or petrified him. Though he's been dead more than fifty years, he looks pretty sharp in his blue suit and striped tie. Years ago when the river flooded Paducah and the funeral home, Speedy was washed away, and "drowned again." Within a week he was found and reinstalled. Now he's famous as a morbid kind of state treasure. If Mrs. Hamock isn't too busy, visitors are more than welcome to see him. She's proud of her late husband's art and can be coaxed into telling other hilarious stories about his sense of humor.

Another 21 miles north on Highway 60 in the tiny town of Burna is the World's Tiniest Itsy-Bitsy Bus Station. Downtown, across the street from Jeannie's Food Market, is a little white clapboard building about the size of a big outhouse with windows and a red, white, and blue Greyhound sign hanging by the door. I guess there's room to sell a ticket. If you need a bus, don't lose faith—the hound will stop wherever there's a sign.

Pennyroyal Region

Tennessee Valley Authority's (TVA) **Land Between the Lakes** (LBL) national recreation area is considered the "Crappie-Fishing Capital of the World," not to mention the huge populations of largemouth and smallmouth bass—an angler's dream-come-true. The Tennessee River was dammed to make Kentucky Lake, and Lake Barkley was formed from the mighty Cumberland River. Together they comprise 220,000 acres of clean, safe water and form a 40-mile-long peninsula the TVA has developed for recreation and education. The Homeplace–1850, for example, is an active living history farm where people in period costumes go about the daily activities of settlers in the mid-nineteenth century. Nearby, a large herd of American bison graze, a sight you can't enjoy in suburbia.

For bird lovers, LBL is one of a scant handful of places where one can get a glimpse of wild bald eagles. In the 1960s poaching and the use of chemicals like DDT reduced the number of breeding eagles to less than 600 pairs, making our national mascot nearly extinct on this continent. The wildlife management people at LBL successfully got the numbers back up by returning raptors to a natural habitat with very little human contact. Ask about eagle and wildlife programs at the Woodlands Nature Center. During the winter, eagle field trips are scheduled for the weekends. Preregistration is necessary, so call (502) 924–5602, extension 238 or 233. Photographers can get close-up pictures of these marvelous creatures in captivity at the Nature Center, or if you're lucky and very patient, in the wild. Enter the park from any direction, Kentucky Highways 68, 94, 641, 24 or in Tennessee from Highways 79 or 76, and go to the Golden Pond Visitor Center for directions and information about the park. You can also call (502) 924–5602.

If you're not camping and are in favor of unusual lodging, try the Round Oak Inn off Highway 68, 1½ miles west of the Barkley State Park Lodge at Devils Elbow; it offers cozy contemporary bed and breakfast facilities. Call (502) 924–5850 for reservations.

The first major town east of the lakes on Highway 68 is Cadiz (pronounced KAYD-eez) named, perhaps, after the hometown of an early Spanish surveyor. Since the creation of Land Between the Lakes, people have said that the name means "gateway" in Spanish, since Cadiz is at the southeastern entrance to the area. Saxophone lovers pay homage here to the inimitable Boots Randolph who was born in Trigg County. (The question is, should a golf course be named after a musician? Poor guy.) Ham lovers must have a meal in town; prize-winning hams are served everywhere. Try Hamtown U.S.A. Restaurant (502–522–3158), open every day, 6:00 A.M. to 9:00 P.M., or take home your own from Broadbent's Food and Gifts (502–522–6674), a big place to buy hams, bacon, sausage, and cheeses, 5 miles east of town near Interstate 24. During the second weekend in October, follow your nose to the Trigg County Country Ham Festival. Nonsoutherners may learn that not all country ham can be safely compared to the salt-drenched tongue of your big brother's hiking boot.

There is something eerie and irresistible about stepping into a person's space and looking at the way their daily life is shaped and revealed by their personal belongings. The **Adsmore** museum in Princeton draws visitors into the lives of its turn-of-the-century residents in that almost-taboo way by presenting the house intact, changing detailed decorations and personal accessories seasonally, and building the tour around stories of the family. The interpretive staff reenacts weddings, birthday parties, and wakes (complete with wailing mourners dressed in period clothes). Details make this place a treat. That the Victorians in Europe were not morally able to utter the phrase "chicken thigh," for example, comes as no surprise when you find that the piano's legs, like a lady's, were always chastely covered with a shawl.

Built in grand late-Victorian style in 1857, Adsmore was fully restored in 1986 by the local library board to which Katherine Garrett, the last family resident, donated the building and its contents. Adsmore could have also been called Collectsmore, for it is furnished lavishly with items from all over the world. Also on the grounds is the Ratliff Gun Shop, a restored 1844 cabin filled with antique tools. Hours are Tuesday through Saturday, 11:00 A.M. to 4:00 P.M., and Sunday, 1:30 to 4:00 P.M. (CST). Admission is $3. Adsmore is on North Jefferson Street in downtown Princeton, which has been called the Natchez of West Kentucky because of its grand homes. From Cadiz, the quickest route is Highway 139 north. From the Land Between the Lakes, take Highway 62, or take Exit 12 from the Western Kentucky Parkway.

For a historic picnic spot, stop at a park one block south of the courthouse at Big Spring, the original settlement's water source and a site where the Cherokees camped on the Trail of Tears. Also noteworthy is the "Black Patch Festival" Princeton hosts in early September to commemorate the times when dark leaf tobacco was harvested in the area in massive quantities. Accompanying this event is a dark and touchy history involving tobacco price wars and the night riders, a movement of farmers (made nationally famous by writers such as Robert Penn Warren) who turned to a sophisticated form of organized violence to ensure the viability of their way of life. Local historians explain the events during the Black Patch tour.

Dark-Leaf Tobacco Barn

Take Highway 91 south from Princeton to downtown Hopkinsville. In the former Federal-style post office building at the corner of East Ninth (Highway 68) and Liberty streets is the **Pennyroyal Area Museum** (502–887–4270), an impressive regional history museum. The main display area is in the huge mail sorting room. Notice the enclosed catwalks overhead, secret vantage points from which postmasters watched postal workers handle the mail, not to enforce efficiency (it was after all, a federal institution), but to prevent workers from stealing cash from the envelopes in a pre-checking account era.

The museum's displays address many facets of the Pennyroyal region's history, from agriculture and the Black Patch wars to reconstructed pioneer bedrooms and an 1898 law office. In the middle of the room sits a beautifully preserved original Mogul wagon, made two blocks away in a large factory that manufactured every imaginable type of wagon. Mogul Wagon Company's ads in the 1920s read "Easy to Pull, Hard to Break" and "Buy a Mogul and Will It to Your Grandson." Railroad and early automobile artifacts compete for your attention with a miniature circus made by John Venable; it is said to have inspired Robert Penn Warren's "Circus in the Attic," the title piece of an early collection of short stories. Museum hours are 8:30 A.M. to 4:30 P.M., Monday through Friday. Admission is $1 for adults.

The Edgar Cayce exhibit is one of the most popular in the museum. The display case contains a few photographs and significant personal objects, like Cayce's dog-eared desk Bible. Cayce, who was born in 1877 in southern Christian County near Beverly, was a strange child who preferred meditating on the Bible to playing baseball. In 1900 after a severe illness, Cayce mysteriously lost his voice. When put under hypnosis by "Hart–The Laugh Man" in 1901, Cayce diagnosed the problem and restored his own voice by using a treatment he discovered during hypnosis. That was the beginning of his career as an internationally known clairvoyant, "the sleeping prophet." He gave 14,256 psychic readings in which he supposedly diagnosed medical problems and predicted world affairs, including natural disasters and economic changes. Today the Association for Research and Enlightenment, based at Virginia Beach where Cayce spent the last twenty years of his life, continues "The Work," as Cayce called it, by providing a library and educational programs related to his readings.

Many of Hopkinsville's visitors from the west pass through town en route to Virginia Beach and stop to see the place where Edgar Cayce and his wife, Gertrude Evans, are buried in the Riverside Cemetery on the north side of town, east of North Virginia Street. Seven miles south of town on the Lafayette Road (Highway 107) in Beverly are Cayce's church, the Liberty Christian Church, which is open to the public, and his school, the Beverly Academy, which is now on private property. If you're a Cayce fan, ask at the museum about other significant sites.

Hopkinsville has done more than any other town in the state to pay tribute to the Native American people who were forced to move from their southeastern homelands across the Mississippi River to Oklahoma on the infamous Trail of Tears during the winter of 1838–39. In town, Cherokee Park marks the site where the more than 13,000 Indians camped and received provisions for their forced migration.

The Trail of Tears Commission, Inc. has developed another park on Pembroke Road (Highway 41) on the west edge of town; it has statues of Cherokee chiefs Whitepath and Fly Smith, who are buried in Hopkinsville. Near the banks of the Little River is a log cabin that serves as an education center. **The Trail of Tears Intertribal Indian Pow Wow** has become an annual event, held during the weekend after Labor Day. Although the recent history of the Native American people is tragic, this public festival is meant to commemorate the beauty and integrity of their culture. The pow wow features Native American crafts, food, storytelling, blow gun demonstrations, and a very competitive Indian dance contest. Contact The Trail of Tears Commission, Inc., P.O. Box 4027, Hopkinsville, KY 42240, or call (502) 886–8033.

In a historic residential district at 317 East Sixteenth Street is **J. B. Crockett's Lone Oak Restaurant,** an upscale eatery with an active ghost. A few years ago the owners of the restaurant hired a security firm to watch the place at night. While keeping watch on the first floor, a young guard heard glass breaking and a female voice calling "Danielle, Danielle." He went upstairs to investigate. He has never told what he saw in the room that was formerly Courtenay Thompson's bedroom, but he ran out into the yard, radioed the main office, and absolutely refused to re-enter the house, even when his supervisor arrived on the scene. Courtenay Hickman Thompson, who grew up in the house, committed suicide in 1920 at the age of twenty-six. Those who have seen her ghost often say she has long brown hair, usually wears a floral dress, and, the wait staff emphasizes, does not like blonde women or profanity. She walks around the house making strange breezes and moving objects like furniture and silverware. An ex-neighbor claims he often saw a woman cleaning windows upstairs after hours.

The restaurant is named after Judge Joseph B. Crockett (a cousin of Davy Crockett) who built the house in 1834. Lunch is served on weekdays from 11:00 A.M. until 2:00 P.M., and dinner is served Monday through Saturday from 5:00 until 10:00 P.M. The meals are exquisite and expensive; everything is fresh and flavorful. Call for reservations or more information at (502) 885–0944 or (800) 621–5798.

The gracious Old South does not end with Crockett's. Melissa and Gary Jones's bed and breakfast, The Oakland Manor (502–885–6400), is truly elegant. From April through December three rooms are available for lodging at the rate of $45 per night. From downtown Hopkinsville, take Canton Pike (Highway 272) to the west, turn left on Newstead Road (Highway 164), and watch for the sign on the left side after about a mile.

As soon as you drive east from Hopkinsville, you are in an area heavily populated by Amish and Mennonite people. Nationally there are about 85,000 Amish, many of whom live in Pennsylvania, Ohio, and Indiana in communities that are being encroached upon by rapidly widening urban edges. Rural Kentucky has become a popular place for Amish families to relocate because the land is beautiful, isolated, and relatively inexpensive. When you visit Amish and Mennonite businesses, keep in mind that they are committed to their way of life in part because they want isolation from the rest of the world. Respect their privacy. Observe their work practices, for they are good stewards of their land and of all their resources. We could stand a little education.

About 6 miles east of town on Highway 68, at a big farmhouse with rock pillars by the driveway, Henry Hoover runs an unadvertised bulk food and farm supply business primarily meant to serve an orthodox community known as "Horse and Buggy Mennonites," folks that have no cars or telephones. He will sell to the public, so stop in if you need flour, cereals, bread, cheese, and so forth. It's a great way to avoid excessive packaging and higher prices due to expensive advertising.

Pete's Custom Saddle Shop is an orderly, productive (secular), one-man leather operation on Highway 68 about 8 miles east of Hopkinsville. In addition to making and refurbishing more than a hundred saddles a year, Russell (Pete) Harry makes holsters, halters, and bridles, not to mention guns, tomahawks, and an occasional painting. Although he's geared primarily to custom work, a few items are always for sale in the shop that will knock your socks off. Pete's original saddle designs range from a sleek bird-hunting saddle to variations on Civil War styles to a western pleasure show saddle with special braces for a local woman who is paralyzed below the shoulders. Even if you are not in need of tack, his stunning work and positive spirit are unique and inspirational. Call him at (502) 886–5448.

One-half-mile east of Pete Harry's place is an Amish harness shop called Leather Works (look for handpainted signs by a road called Vaughns Grove on the north side of the highway), where a young farmer named Wayne Zimmerman makes and repairs leather tack of all kinds, except saddles. That his specialty is harnesses is no accident. Except for very heavy work like plowing, he and many Amish and Mennonite farmers in the area work with mule teams. The shop is small and he does not keep much in stock, but, if you are interested in placing an order or just in seeing the operation, stop by. Hours are by chance.

One mile past Wayne Zimmerman's place is Fairview, a tiny rural town you can't miss, thanks to the Jefferson Davis Monument State Shrine looming overhead at the height of 351 feet. From miles away in any direction the incongruous tower, said to be the tallest concrete-cast obelisk in the world, is visible poking into the sky. During the summer you can ride an elevator to the top of the monument. Jefferson Davis, the first and only president of the Confederate States, was born in March of 1808 in a house called Wayfarers Rest on the site of what is now the Bethel Baptist Church in Fairview. Adjacent to the monument is the Zimmerman Farms produce stand, run by Wayne Zimmerman's brothers. From late May to mid-October you can buy delicious, organically grown fruits and vegetables. You can trust the Amish when it comes to wholesome, flavorful produce.

At Elkton, 8 miles east of Fairview, take Highway 181 south for about 10 miles and look to the right for Schlabach's Bakery, an Amish bakery specializing in satisfaction. Their sourdough bread, sweet rolls, pies, cakes, cookies, and yes, even granola are delicious and always fresh. Hours are 8:00 A.M. to 5:00 P.M. every day but Thursday and Sunday. Although the owner is Abe Schlabach (502–265–2075), you'll be more likely to meet one of his bakers who live nearby.

To illustrate how these Amish (there are many kinds of Amish communities) adjust their lives to both the community rules and the modern world, let me tell you how Betty Miller gets to work at the bakery every morning. Her community uses tractors and horse and buggy rigs, but not cars or bicycles. If she were male, she might hop on her Massey Ferguson and drive, and if she were a child, she might sprint. Instead, she gets on her small tractor (a riding lawnmower) and commutes through yards and along the shoulder of the highway. Some communities won't use any vehicle with rubber tires, so they own steel-wheeled tractors. Other communities of plain people have cars and trucks but insist that they be painted black, even the chrome parts. Others have brightly colored cars and attend graduate school. And, at the other extreme, orthodox communities use only horses and oxen.

Another mile or so south, at the intersection of Highways 181 and 848, is the **Penchem Tack Store,** a large Amish tack and farm supply store also used by the general public. John H. Yoders and his sons work in the leather shop in the basement while another family member tends to retail sales upstairs. It's a great place to browse, especially if you're in the market for good functional suspenders, straw work hats, Redwing shoes, veterinary supplies, tack (commercially and locally made), or just a soft drink and a candy bar. Call (502) 483–2314.

If Amish men are among the best leatherworkers, the women have always been known for the fine art of quilting. Grandma's Cupboard is an informal sales outlet for women who make quilts, hooked rugs, and woven runners. From Penchem's, go left (east) on Highway 848 to Highway 79; turn left (north) and stop at the second house on the right. Elmer and Mary Hochstetler have recently closed their large dairy business because none of their male children stayed on the family farm. He still farms while she babysits, makes quilts, and runs the small sales operation. In the little building by the road (an ex–gas station) the family has a small bookstore full of Amish, Mennonite, and other Christian printed materials. With the help of other local quilters, Mary Hochstetler can make almost any type of quilt to order and usually has exquisite finished pieces for sale. Tell her and her daughters that I said hello. You can call Mary at (502) 483–2461.

If you are in the area in early summer and get that unbearable craving for strawberries, call the local strawberry kings—Emmett Walton in Allensville (502–265–5597) or Tommy Borders near Elkton (502–265–5770)—to see if they are open for U-Pick. They'll direct you to the field on which you may sweetly graze.

Due south on either Highway 79 or 41, nestled right next to the Tennessee border, is the town of Guthrie, birthplace of Robert Penn Warren, poet laureate of the United States and Pulitzer prize winner for both poetry and fiction. For those who have read his work, it is enriching to walk the streets and drive by the endless fields, an environment that obviously influenced his writing. Once in town, if you want details or if you'd like to tour the house in which Robert Penn Warren was born, contact Mrs. Dean Moore (502–483–2683).

Libby's Steakhouse & Entertainment Center is probably the biggest restaurant building you have ever seen, and it's bound to have the widest variety of entertainment you can imagine *inside* a restaurant—horse shows, live FM music broadcasts, professional Nashville country music performances, open dances, rodeos, thumb pickin' contests, parties, and even beauty pageants. It's a "family restaurant," so no alcohol is served, but they offer a full Southern menu. The 48-ounce "West Texas Slab" rib loin steak is yours free if you can clean your plate. Libby's opens at 5:00 P.M. on Friday and Saturday only (502–265–2630). Find the place on Highway 68 at its junction with Highway 1309 in Daysville, between Elkton and Russellville.

On Highway 79, about halfway between Guthrie and Russellville, stop in Allensville at a classy bed and breakfast called The Pepper Place. Take Highway 102 east toward town and watch for the sign in front of a large, blue clapboard house, circa 1864, with an inviting wraparound porch. Three rooms are available for lodging, and the whole house is available for weddings, receptions, and catered meals. Many of the period antiques in The Pepper Place are for sale. Write Dr. Craig, P.O. Box 95, Allensville, KY 42204, or call (502) 265–9859 for reservations.

The Southern Deposit Bank in downtown Russellville on the corner of Main and Sixth streets is the scene of a great crime—the Jesse James gang's first out-of-state robbery. Prior to that day the gang was a handful of local hoodlums. On May 20, 1868 the gang held up the bank for $9,000, shot and wounded bank president N. Long, and galloped away to join the ranks of America's famous federal fugitives. (What Jesse didn't know was that there were $50,000 more in the vault.) Today the bank has been restored into a classy, crime-free apartment building.

If you need a place to spend the night in Russellville, try the restored 1824 home of George Washington's third cousin, John Whiting Washington. The Washington House is a bed and breakfast with five rooms. Contact Roy Gill, 283 West Ninth Street, Russellville, KY 42276, or call (502) 726–7608 or 726–3093.

East of Russellville on Highway 68 on the west edge of the town of Auburn is a Mennonite general store called **The Dutch House** (502–542–7750). Proprietor Joe Miller keeps the place well stocked with organic bulk foods, fresh breads, rolls, cookies, and cakes from local bakeries, quilts, hooked rugs, Amish cheeses, and fabric and notions, among other things. If you aren't hungry when you stop, you will be after you peruse the shelves. Hours are Monday through Saturday, 9:00 A.M. to 5:00 or 6:00 P.M. Ask Joe Miller about local auctions. The Mennonite churches put on fantastic fund-raisers featuring great food (like homemade noodles), quality farm equipment, furniture, quilts, and exotic items like bottled vanilla from Mission trips to Haiti.

Within shouting distance is the Auburn Guest House, a five-room bed and breakfast in a Colonial-style mansion filled to the brim with antiques. Owners David and Joy Williams insist on serving a full (and I mean *full*) Southern-style morning meal. For reservations write them at 421 West Main Street, Auburn, KY 42206, or call after 3:00 P.M. at (502) 542–6019. The guest house is within walking distance of a number of antique shops downtown.

Three miles east on Highway 68 is **Shakertown at South Union,** now a small museum marking the site of a once-thriving village comprising more than 6,000 acres and 200 buildings. Members of the United Society of Believers in Christ's Second Appearance, more commonly known as Shakers, lived at the South Union community from 1807 until 1922. They supported themselves with sophisticated enterprises in garden seed, fruit preserves, fine colorful silk handkerchiefs, and, of course, farming. They also ran a large steam-powered mill, hired some of Kentucky's first purebred bulls for stud all over the state, and built and leased out (to the World) a train depot, post office/general store, and tavern. Had they survived, I feel sure they'd be raising beefalo and programming computers.

The forty-room building that now serves as the main museum was the Center House, a dwelling complete with kitchen, communal dining room, and bedrooms, men on one side, women on the other. The building fulfills your basic expectations of a Shaker structure, but in a slightly showier way; some of the trim boards are beaded, there are several nooks for clocks, the first-floor window casings flare in, and arches abound. From the woodstoves to the cooking utensils to hat molds, South Union is filled with original Shaker objects, not reproductions. Even the brick-dust and mustard-ochre stains on the woodwork are original (let's hear it for organic paint!).

The museum and gift shop are open from April 1 through November, Monday through Friday from 9:00 A.M. to 5:00 P.M.,

Shakertown at South Union

and Sunday from 1:00 to 5:00 P.M. Admission is $2.50 for adults and $1 for children ages six through twelve. Call (502) 542–4167 for further information. One mile east of the museum is Highway 73. Turn left (south) and go ½-mile to the South Union Antique Mall and Post Office (501–542–6757), established April 1, 1826. Next door, the Sisters' Shop, another original Shaker building, is also being used as an antique shop. Hours are 10:00 A.M. to 5:00 P.M., Monday through Saturday (502–542–7815). For updated schedules of festivals and events, write Shakertown, South Union, KY 42283.

Yellow Banks, Green River

Daddy, won't you take me back to Muhlenberg County,
Down by the Green River where Paradise lay.
I'm sorry my son but you're too late in askin',
Mr. Peabody's coal train has hauled it away.

John Prine's famous lyrics give us a glimpse of Muhlenberg County's history, and traveling through the area gives us an update. "Paradise" is an enormous steam-generating power plant, the largest of its kind when it was built in the late 1950s. The county has not been all hauled away, but you may think they're trying to do so when you see some of the monstrous earth-moving machines in the surface mines visible from several major roads. (The term "strip mine" for "surface mine" is taboo around here, but it's also sadly accurate.) Even driving through it, you'll believe that this county had been the largest coal-producing county in the United States for twenty-three consecutive years until EPA regulations reduced the market for the area's high-sulphur coal.

Aside from coal, great country music is the area's claim to fame. In front of the City Building in Central City is a monument to the town's native sons, Phil and Don Everly. Every Labor Day weekend the Everly Brothers and more than 10,000 fans come to town for a benefit concert called the "Everly Brothers Central City Music Festival," the proceeds of which go to music scholarships and other community projects. One of the favorite events is the International Thumbpicking Contest in honor of Merle Travis. Call for festival information at (502) 754–9603.

Greenville, south of the Western Kentucky Parkway on Highways 62 or 189, is home to several one-of-a-kinds. One is the House of Onyx, a mega-mart of gemstones that promotes investment in precious rocks and discourages trust in the banking system. Beyond inventory and prices, their literature consists of an odd combination of claims that theirs is a real, honest business and fortune-cookie-type moralistic quotes. One's curiosity is certainly piqued. The business is geared primarily toward the wholesale and mail-order markets, but if you are in town on a weekday between 9:00 A.M. and 4:30 P.M., stop in for a tour of the retail showroom. You'll be astounded by the rows of cases of rubies, sapphires, pearls, and myriad other stones. Though there is no sign, the office is in the Aaron Building at 120 North Main Street in downtown Greenville. Ring the doorbell and explain your interest, or call ahead for an appointment at (502) 338–2363.

A little known fact: Greenville is home of the State Championship Washer Pitching Play-offs. Washer pitching is the rural American version of the ancient game of "quoits," which is related to horseshoe pitching. In the heat of late summer, the play-offs are held at the Greenville Municipal Ball Park. You'll get a schedule for the event if and when you win a district blue ribbon.

If you plan to dine or spend a night in the area, take Highway 431 south from Central City to the **Lake Malone Inn** (502–657–2121) in Dunmor. In addition to the hotel and big restaurant, the Inn houses the studio of Glenn Robertson, a painter specializing in African wildlife. Fishing is fantastic in the Lake Malone State Park. The 788-acre lake is surrounded by a 388-acre park laced with middle-aged pine forests and sandstone bluffs and caves where the Jesse James gang supposedly hid. (Jesse James is to west Kentucky what Daniel Boone is to the central and eastern parts—both hid everywhere, carved their initials on every historic tree and building, and are still receiving royalties for their freely interpreted deeds.)

What do bluegrass music, Scotch taxidermy, and bar-b-q mutton have in common? The Owensboro area. If you are approaching the area by the Bluegrass Parkway and still need convincing that Kentucky is far from mundane, head north on the Green River Parkway and take Exit 69 to the tiny town of Dundee. When you get into town, keep your eyes to the sky. Standing stiffly above the Masonic lodge is a stuffed goat, imported almost one hundred years ago from Dundee, Scotland. The town, which was once called Hines Mill, changed its name to commemorate this oddity.

On to the self-proclaimed "Bar-B-Q Capital of the World" and the third largest city in the state, Owensboro. In this town, where there's smoke, there's barbecue. Initiate yourself by eating at one of the many "smoking" restaurants, ranging from a humble joint called George's Bar-B-Q, where you can sample one version of honest-to-goodness Kentucky Burgoo (a super-hearty meat and veggie stew that originated in Wales and came here via Virginia with the pioneers) to the famous Moonlite Bar-B-Q Inn (502–684–8143), a huge restaurant west of town on Parrish Street where the barbecue is all hickory-pit cooked. Hours are 9:00 A.M. to 9:00 P.M., Monday through Saturday, and 10:00 A.M. to 3:00 P.M. on Sunday.

In mid-May Owensboro comes alive for the International Bar-B-Q Festival, during which time the local folks compete fiercely for culinary titles. My friend's father, "Pop Beers," concocted a darn-good recipe for barbecue chicken that has won three festival championships. Because this generous soul has given me permission to give you his secret recipe, I hereby command you to sensitize your palate before participating in the festival. I quote:

Bring the following barbecue sauce ingredients to a rapid boil on medium-high heat:

1 stick butter
1 big lemon
1 tablespoon Worcestershire sauce
1 tablespoon soy sauce
5 shakes Tabasco sauce
1 teaspoon black pepper
1 teaspoon paprika
1 teaspoon garlic powder
1 teaspoon Accent meat tenderizer
1 teaspoon poultry seasoning

Cook the sauce until a brown scum forms and then goes away. Let cool and use. Won't spoil if kept. Makes enough sauce for three 3-pound chickens. To use, cut fat (NOT skin) off a whole roasting chicken. Grill on one side for 30 minutes, turn and repeat. Then turn the chicken again, baste, and grill for 15 minutes; turn again and repeat. Eat.

Because downtown Owensboro is proud of its historic buildings, the Historical Society and Preservation Alliance (502–926–1100) gives free tours on request. My favorite landmark in town is a **sassafras tree** in the front yard of the E. M. Ford & Company on the corner of Frederica and Maple streets. At a height of 100 feet and a circumference of 16 feet, this 250–300-year-old droopy-armed beauty is registered by the American Forestry Association as being the largest of its kind in the country and probably in the world. A Mrs. Rash saved the tree from the merciless highway department by planting herself at the base of the trunk with a shotgun in hand. She then pulled political strings and the governor immediately installed a retaining wall and lightning rod. (I'll bet Earth First! could use a Mrs. Rash.)

On Griffith Avenue is the **Owensboro Area Museum,** a natural science and history extravaganza containing everything from live reptiles to a seventy-five-seat planetarium, a tobacco store figure of Punch, and dinosaur replicas. Kids and uninhibited adults love this place. Though it is said that the museum started in a church building in 1966, the truth is that it began somewhat earlier in local storyteller and natural historian Joe Ford's backyard playhouse, where he stockpiled insects, rocks, and snakeskins, some of which are still in the museum collection. Hours are Monday through Friday, 8:00 A.M. to 4:00 P.M., and on weekends from 1:00 to 4:00 P.M. Call (502) 683–0296.

Owensboro's International Bluegrass Music Association Fanfest is geared toward preservation and modern bluegrass music and always involves some of the world's best bluegrass musicians. Bluegrass and banjo fanatics must make plans to be at English Park, overlooking the Ohio River, in mid-September. Contact Dan Hays (502–684–9025) or the Tourist Commission (502–926–1100) for details. An International Bluegrass Music Museum is soon to be built near the River Park Center. They're serious—the board has already inducted members into the Bluegrass Music Hall of Honor. The Owensboro Community College Inter-Tribal Indian Festival held annually in early October includes an intertribal pow wow, dancing, and Native American food and crafts. The pow wow is open to the public. Contact Bruce Beck at (502) 686–4400 for more information.

One of Kentucky's largest fine art museums, **The Owensboro**

Museum of Fine Art at 901 Frederica Street has an impressive permanent collection of works from eighteenth-, nineteenth-, and twentieth-century American, English, and French masters and a decorative arts collection of American, European, and Asian objects from the fifteenth to nineteenth centuries. Their consistent exhibition of Kentucky and regional artists is laudable. For example, they regularly organize national touring exhibitions of traditional Appalachian art. Hours are Monday through Friday, 10:00 A.M. to 4:00 P.M., and weekends from 1:00 to 4:00 P.M. Admission is free. Call (502) 685–3181.

You may find that rest can also be found in activity. Do tennis (indoor and out), racquetball, swimming, horseback riding, fishing, canoeing, weight lifting, and sauna strike you as heavy labor? Joan Ramey-Ford, manager of Ramey Tennis Schools, has opened her "Friendly Farms and Our Tennis House" facilities to all appreciative visitors. Several cottages are now available for bed and breakfast lodging at $50 per night for one person and $5 for each additional guest; this includes Ms. Ford's athlete's breakfast. Call (502) 771–5590 or 771–4723 for reservations or more information.

WeatherBerry Bed and Breakfast at 2731 Second Street West offers country-style lodging very close to town. For $50 to $70 a night, depending on the size of the room, you get a private bath and a grand Kentucky-style breakfast or a more moderate "healthful" repast. The previous residents of the impressive 1840 farmhouse had a vineyard and collected weather information for the National Weather Bureau, hence the name WeatherBerry. Call (502) 684–US60 for reservations.

In all cultures, people set time aside to make retreats—quiet time for contemplation away from the bustle of everyday life. Whether or not you are Catholic or connected to any church or creed in any way, **Mount Saint Joseph Center and Community of Ursuline Sisters** offers a quiet, respectful atmosphere to those of us yearning for space and time to absorb (or forget) life. Aside from retreats, the center offers all kinds of religious, cultural, and social programs. Call (502) 229–4103 for information. Take Parrish Avenue (Highway 81) west out of town until it turns south; take Highway 56 to West Louisville, turn right (west) on Highway 815, and look for the sign within 2 miles. Go in the Maple Mount Farm entrance, find the Mother House, and ask to see the center's museum. Sister Emma Cecilia Busam will guide you through the museum artifacts, which range from desks of the founders to gifts from foreign missions, musical instruments, religious articles, books, and displays like "The Madonna Room," which houses a collection of reproductions of famous European Madonna paintings. You'll enjoy seeing odd artifacts like the pair of antique and modern "host-making utensils." For a time, the sisters here manufactured "host" or "altar breads," the flat white-flour wafers used in communion services. The old wafer maker is made of heavy cast iron and was used over an open fire while the newer one resembles an electric waffle iron one might use to make breakfast. The non-Catholic visitor is in for a real education.

From Mount Saint Joseph, take a westward drive on Highway 56 for 11 miles to the **Diamond Lake Catfish Farm**. Statewide catfish farming is on the rise because reclaimed surface mines are required to have settling ponds, which turn out to be great places for raising fish. This farm is a successful, sophisticated business that is more than happy to show people around. During the summer, visitors ride a tram to see the whole operation. Open daily during business hours. Call (502) 229–4961.

After the fish farm tour, you may be curious to know how the "produce" tastes. The Windy Hollow Restaurant and Museum (502–785–4088) has a famous catfish buffet on Friday and Saturday from 4:00 to 8:30 P.M. and a big country ham breakfast buffet on Sunday from 7:00 A.M. to 1:30 P.M. From Owensboro, follow Highway 81 southwest to Windy Hollow Road and follow the signs.

The **John James Audubon State Park** is in Henderson, about 20 miles west of Owensboro off Highway 54. Although Audubon is the most famous American painter of birds, he was a failure as a businessman. While he lived in this area, from 1810 to 1820, Audubon got involved in several entrepreneurial projects, all of which failed because, instead of working, he spent his days in search of rare birds. He dragged his poor family all over the South while he painted and searched for a publisher. Eventually he found an engraver in London, England, who printed his 435 hand-colored plates as *Birds of America*. Originals from the folio edition are on display in the Audubon Memorial and Nature Museum as are many of Audubon's original paintings. Another treasure in the museum is a rare 3-by-5-inch daguerrotype of the elderly Audubon. Hours are 9:00 A.M. to 5:00 P.M. daily from April 1 through October 31; from November through March, except in January when it is completely closed, the museum is open only on weekends.

In addition to the usual state park recreational facilities, the whole northern half of the park was donated as a nature preserve, with the stipulation that it be treated as a bird sanctuary and that the old-growth beech and sugar maple woods be preserved. Ask the park naturalist for information on the wild and amazing flora and fauna that can be seen. The park also sponsors spring and fall migration bird walks. Call (502) 562–2886 for more information.

INDEX

About the Author

An independent writer, ceramic sculptor, and farmer-in-the-making, Zoé Strecker spends her time scribbling, moving dirt, playing with fire, and worrying about the weather at her farm near the Kentucky River in Mercer County. She finds the not-so-quiet rural life loaded with the harsh and beautiful mysteries of reality. Zoé's writing—poetry, essays, and short fiction—appears sporadically in regional and national publications. Her ceramic sculpture and architectural tile is exhibited and puzzled over throughout the country. She graduated from Iowa's Grinnell College in 1988, and has since relished her tumultuous self-unemployment.